**GÚNA NUA THEATRE** AND **PLAN B**

# unravelling the ribbon

## BY **MARY KELLY** AND **MAUREEN WHITE**

| | |
|---|---|
| **ROSE** | Mary Kelly |
| **LOLA** | Eleanor Methven |
| **LYNDSEY** | Georgina Miller |

| | |
|---|---|
| **Director** | Maureen White |
| **Set and Costume Designer** | Liz Cullinane |
| **Lighting Designer** | Tina MacHugh |
| **Music and Sound Designers** | Denis Clohessy and Carl Kennedy |
| **Production Manager** | Bianca Moore |
| **Stage Director** | Miriam Duffy |
| **Stage Manager** | Petra Hjortsberg |
| **Photography** | Ros Kavanagh |
| **Graphic Designer** | Kieran Brennan at Revision Design |
| **Sponsorship Co-ordinator** | Katy Davis |
| **Chief Electrician** | Lisa Mahony |
| **Set Construction** | Jim Carson |
| **PR** | Kate Bowe PR |
| **Production Interns** | Shannon Klousia |
| | Kendall Sherwood |

For Plan B Productions

| **Directors** | Mary Kelly and Maureen White |
|---|---|

For Gúna Nua Theatre

| **Artistic Directors** | Paul Meade and David Parnell |
|---|---|
| **Administrator** | Tara Furlong |

**First performed at Project Arts Centre, Dublin,
on Wednesday 24 October 2007**

*Unravelling the Ribbon* was presented in association with
Action Breast Cancer (a programme of the Irish Cancer Society), and proudly
sponsored by Avon Cosmetics Breast Cancer Crusade

# COMPANY BIOGRAPHIES

**Denis Clohessy** (Music and Sound Designer) Denis has composed music and sound for more than sixty theatre and dance productions, including: *Woman and Scarecrow*, *The Crucible* and *Julius Caesar* (Abbey Theatre); *Is This About Sex?*, *Attempts on Her Life*, *Don Carlos* and *Dream of Autumn* (Rough Magic); *Festen* (Gate Theatre); *The Pride of Parnell Street* (Fishamble); *Titus Andronicus*, *Shutter*, *La Musica* and *Fando and Lis* (Siren Productions); *Sleeping Beauty* and *Underneath the Lintel* (Landmark); *Mushroom*, *Rashomon*, *The Dream of a Summer Day* and *The Crock of Gold* (Storytellers); *Hysteria*, *Family Stories* and *Tejas Verdes* (B*Spoke); *Bones*, *Talking to Terrorists* and *Operation Easter* (Calypso); *Last Call*, *Devotion* and *How High Is Up* (TEAM theatre); *Splendour*, *Winter* and *The System* (RAW). Denis has also composed for a number of short films including the European Academy Award-winning *Undressing My Mother* and *Useless Dog* (Venom Films), for which he won Best Soundtrack at the 2005 European Short Film Biennale.

**Liz Cullinane** (Set and Costume Designer) Liz has worked in many areas of visual art, beginning as a theatre designer in 1984 with Cork-based Graffiti Theatre Company. Her work includes: *The Hamster Wheel*, *Bondagers* and *A Wife a Dog a Maple Tree* (Charabanc, Belfast); *Combattimenti*, opera battles for Opera Theatre Company; *How Many Miles to Babylon* (Lyric Belfast); *Keely and Du* (Olympia); *Low in the Dark* and *Big Mom* (The Project). She has been based in Belfast for the past twelve years where she has diversified into film, carnival arts and art direction for television commercials. Film work includes: *Gort na gCnamh*, *Room*, *Picnic*, *A Rap at the Door* and *Being Special*. Liz has designed costumes for Belfast Community Circus shows and extensive carnival design with The Beat, including large-scale puppets. Most recently Liz has designed *Babyrave*, a touring event for Young at Art that had great success at Adelaide, Edinburgh and Belfast children's festivals.

**Miriam Duffy** (Stage Director) Miriam works as a stage director, production manager and designer/prop maker. She has previously worked with Gúna Nua as Stage Director for the Dublin run of *Trousers*, and was production manager on its Irish tour. As a stage director she has worked with most Irish theatre and dance companies, including, most recently: *Roberto Zucco* (Bedrock); *The Constant Wife* (Gate Theatre at Spoleto Festival, South Carolina); and Trevor Knight's *Slat* for Galway Arts Festival, for which she was also production manager. Set and costume design credits include: *A Picture of Me* (The Ark); *The Cambria* and *Vive La* for Donal O'Kelly; *Dedalus Lounge* (Samuel Beckett Centre/DFF); *Tanks a lot!* (Barabbas). Prop and special effects design credits include: *Annabel's Star* (The Ark); *Dog*, *Hupnous* and *Out the Back Door* (Barabbas); *Coraline* (Puca Puppets); *Hansel and Gretel*, *The BFG* (Civic Theatre).

**Petra Hjortsberg** (Stage Manager) With a background in graphic design, photography and set design, Petra's Irish credits include: costumes on *Coyote on a Fence* (Purple Heart Theatre Company); photography and graphic design for *p.ubu* (Articulate Anatomy); costumes on *Lonely Hearts* (Observatory Lane Theatre Company); and set design on *The Little Prince* (Mutations Theatre Company). Since 2007, she has also worked as a stage manager, most recently on *Mushroom* for Storytellers Theatre Company.

**Mary Kelly** (Co-Writer, *Rose*) Mary is an actor and a writer. She graduated from the Gaiety School of Acting in 2002 with *Requiem for Lena* (dir. Veronica Coburn). Since then she has written and performed her own work, *One for Sorrow* and *Two for a Girl* (dir. Maureen White), which had nationwide success. Other theatre includes: *Black Ice* (dir. Martin Murphy); *Jack Fell Down* (dir. Mark O'Brien); *Lonely Hearts* (dir. Paul Keely); *The One Project* (dir. Gavin Quinn); *Kandachime* (Japanese dance company); *Shooters* (dir. John O'Brien, Purple Heart); *The Little Mermaid* (dir. Zoe Seaton). Television and radio work includes: *Fair City*, *Mayday* (Radio – Veronica Coburn). Mary is a co-founder of Plan B Productions. *Unravelling the Ribbon* is their first production.

**Carl Kennedy** (Sound Designer) Carl composed and worked as a musician for singer-songwriter Sarah Lynch in Galway, and from there began composing and sound designing for theatre. Theatre includes: *One Last White Horse*, co-designed with Ian Kehoe for Galway Youth Theatre; Activate Youth Theatre's *Ideal Homes Show*, by Ciaran Fitzpatrick; and Sligo Youth Theatre's production of *The Crucible*. He was composer/sound designer on *They Never Froze Walt Disney* by Jody O'Neill, which was part of the Cork Midsummer Festival 2007, and most recently the Granary New Directors Festival production of *Howie the Rookie*.

**Tina MacHugh** (Lighting Designer) Tina's theatre work in Ireland includes: *Hedda Gabler*, *The Playboy of the Western World*, *Doldrum Bay*, *Done Up Like a Kipper*, *On Such As We*, *The Hunt for Red Willie* (Abbey and Peacock Theatres); *Ubu Roi* (Galway Arts Festival); *The Whisperers* (Rough Magic); as well as productions for the Gate, Prime Cut, Kilkenny Festival and Druid Theatre. Work in the UK includes: *Grapes of Wrath* (Clwyd Theatr Cymru); *The Way Home*, *Paradise Bound* (Liverpool Everyman); *The Hypochondriac* (Belgrade Theatre Coventry); *When Harry Met Sally* (UK Tour); *Mrs Pat* (York Theatre Royal); *Sweeney Todd* (Derby Playhouse); *Nixon's Nixon* (West End); *Midden* (Hampstead); *Our Father* (Almeida); *The Tempest*, *Love in the Wood*, *The Comedy of Errors*, *Henry VI*, *The Phoenician Women*, *Shadows* (RSC); *Yard Girl*, *Live like Pigs* (Royal Court); *The Machine Wreckers*, *Guiding Star*, and *Rutherford and Son* (National Theatre, London). Tina was nominated for an Olivier Award for *Rutherford and Son* and *Ghosts*. Opera credits include: *Orlando*, *Apollo and Hyacinthus*, *Vera of Las Vegas*, *Katya Kabanova* (Opera Theatre Company); *Idomeneo* with Placido Domingo (Los Angeles Opera); *Il Re Pastore* (Scottish Opera); *Domeneo de Vlaamse* (Antwerp); *Falstaff* (English Touring Opera). Dance credits include work with DV8, Adventures in Motion Pictures, English National Ballet, Rambert Dance Company, Houston Ballet and Fabulous Beast.

**Eleanor Methven** (*Lola*) In 1983 Eleanor co-founded the award-winning Charabanc Theatre Company, with whom she toured internationally for several years, and remained as Co-Artistic Director until 1995. In 1993 she received an EMA Best Actress award for her work with Charabanc. In 2003 she received an Irish Times/ESB Best Actress Award for her portrayal of Maggie Mundy in *Dancing at Lughnasa*. She received an IFTA nomination in 2005 as Best Supporting Actress, for her role as Eileen Kirwan in the RTE/Saffron Pictures television series *Love is a Drug*. Recent theatre credits include: *Pentecost* and *Don Carlos* (Rough Magic); *The Barbaric Comedies*, *Tartuffe*, *The Wild Duck*, *The Shape of Metal*, *Hamlet*, *Homeland* and *Saved* (Abbey and Peacock Theatres); *Weddins, Weeins and Wakes*, *The Factory Girls*, *Conversations on a Homecoming* and *The Shadow of a Gunman* (Lyric Belfast); *Simpatico* and *Scenes from fhe Big Picture* (Prime Cut); *Dancing at Lughnasa* (An Grianan Productions); *Jane Eyre* (Gate); *All's Well That Ends Well* (Classic Stage Ireland); *The Year of the Hiker* (Druid). Film work includes: *The Snapper*, *The*

*Disappearance of Finbar*, *The Boxer*, *Just in Time*, *Mad About Mambo*, *A Love Divided*, *Disco Pigs*, *Becoming Jane*. Television work includes: *Falling for a Dancer*, *The Ambassador*, *D.D.U.*, *Baby Wars*, *The Return*, *Love is a Drug*, *The Clinic*.

**Georgina Miller** (*Lyndsey*) Georgina trained at the Gaiety School of Acting, Dublin. Theatre credits include: *The Big House* (Abbey Theatre); *The Snow Queen* (Graffiti); *Lovers*, *Where He Lies* (Island); *Action* (Locus); *One Last White Horse*, *At the Black Pig's Dyke*, *Wild Harvest* (MIDAS). Television work includes: *Pure Mule* (Eden Films) and *Trouble in Paradise* (Great Western Films). Georgina has worked extensively with Crazydog Audio Theatre Company and has performed in a number of radio plays for RTE Radio 1 including *Infidel*, *Danny's Girl*, *Jumping for Joy* and *The Strange Case of the Great Crested Canary*.

**Bianca Moore** (Production Manager) Bianca is a freelance production manager, stage manager and prop maker. She has recently worked as a production manager on *The Pride of Parnell Street* (Fishamble); *Mushroom* (Storytellers); *The Townlands of Brazil* (Axis); and *Trousers* (Gúna Nua and Civic Theatre). Other production management credits include: *The Crock of Gold* and *The Red Hot Runaways* (Storytellers and Civic Theatre), and *A Dream of a Summer Day* (Storytellers). Recent stage management credits include: *Monged* (Liverpool Arts Festival), and *Whereabouts* (both Fishamble productions); and *Tanks A Lot!* (Barabbas). Bianca designed and made the giant heads for *The BFG* (Civic Theatre), and the marshmallow furniture for *Tanks A Lot!*. She has also made various props for the Abbey, Barnstorm, the Ark, and Gaiety Pantomimes. Production design credits include: *The Dock Brief*, *So Long Sleeping Beauty*, *One for Sorrow*, *Just a Little One*, *Sue Collins is Only Gorgeous*, *Two for a Girl* and *The Twelve Pound Look* (Bewleys Café Theatre).

**Maureen White** (Co-Writer, Director) Maureen White is a director, writer, teacher, and co-founder of Canada's Nightwood Theatre (with Kim Renders, Mary Vingoe and Cynthia Grant). Maureen's work in Canada includes: writer/performer in *This Is For You Anna*, a collective which toured Ontario Theatres and was part of the Du Maurier International Festival, Toronto; Director of the Dora Mavor Moore award-winning production of *The Stone Angel* (Theatre Passe Muraille); the award-winning children's show *Thin Ice* (Theatre Direct); the English premiere of *Aurelie, Ma Soeur* (Centaur Theatre and National Arts Centre); *The Arab's Mouth* and *The Clichettes* (Factory Theatre). In addition, she has worked with Nightwood Theatre to initiate the Groundswell Festival, Canada's national play development program for new works by women, now in its twenty-third year. Directing work in Ireland includes: *Pagliacci/Frankies*, *Combattimenti*, *Bitter Fruit*, *Sensational* (Opera Theatre Company); *Bondagers* (Charabanc Theatre); *Fear of Feathers* (Andrews Lane Theatre). She was also dramaturg on *Play About My Dad* by Michelle Read, and *The Lament for Arthur Cleary* by Dermot Bolger. Previous published work includes: *This Is For You Anna* (co-written with Anne Marie MacDonald, Suzanne Khuri and Banuta Rubess). Maureen White is the first-year acting teacher for the Gaiety School of Acting.

## GÚNA NUA THEATRE

*'one of Ireland's most original, even radical, companies'* The Sunday Tribune

Gúna Nua Theatre is an independent production company based in Dublin and founded by Paul Meade and David Parnell. The company has a commitment to devising new work for the stage, to developing new Irish writing, and to touring nationally and internationally. Previous productions include the new plays *Trousers* (Project Cube, national tour, and E59E Theatres, New York; in co-production with Civic Theatre); *Thesis* (in co-production with Civic Theatre); *Skin Deep* (Project Dublin), which won the Stewart Parker Award, and an Irish Theatre Awards Nomination for Judges Special Award; *Taste* (Andrews Lane, Dublin); *Scenes from a Water Cooler* (Project Cube, Andrews Lane, national tour and Tron, Glasgow), which won the award for Best Production at the Dublin Fringe Festival 2001; and *Four Storeys* (Project Dublin). Other productions include *Hamlet* (Project and national tour); *Dinner With Friends* (Andrews Lane, in co-production with Lane Productions); *The Real Thing* (Andrews Lane, in co-production with Andrews Lane); *The Importance of Being Earnest* (Civic Theatre and Dublin Tour; in co-production with Civic Theatre); and *Burn This* (Dublin Fringe, 2000). Gúna Nua is grant-aided by the Arts Council and Dublin City Council.

## PLAN B PRODUCTIONS

Collaboration between Maureen White and Mary Kelly on *Unravelling the Ribbon* began when Maureen directed Mary in *One For Sorrow* and *Two For A Girl*. Maureen White and Mary Kelly co-formed Plan B Productions and *Unravelling the Ribbon* is their first production.

### A Note from Plan B Productions

*Unravelling the Ribbon* has been a project full of invigorating encounters. To the women we met in Dublin, Cork, Waterford and Mullingar – who shared their experiences of breast cancer with us – thank you. Thanks also to Paul Meade and David Parnell for reading early drafts and giving gentle nudges at just the right times, and to the amazing Tara Furlong for making everything easy.

Thanks to Abby Langtry, Patrick Sutton, Kieran Brennan and Judith Wojtowicz for backing us from the start. A very special thanks to Gúna Nua for co-producing the play with Plan B Productions – it's been such a pleasure.

## FOR PROJECT ARTS CENTRE

**Willie White**   Artistic Director
**Niamh O'Donnell**   General Manager
**Joseph Collins**   Technical Manager
**Annette Devoy**   Administrator
**Carmel Mackey**   House Manager
**Aisling McGrane**   Press Officer
**Kate McSweeney**   Finance & Accounts Officer
**Rachel Ní Chuinn**   Box Office
**Ross Ó Corráin**   Marketing Officer
**David Quinlan**   Production Manager
**Joe Roch**   Bar Supervisor
**Siobhan Shortt**   Box Office Co-ordinator

Gúna Nua and Plan B Productions are grateful to the following for their assistance with this production:

Gavin Denn, Elayne Tighe, Lisa Lambe, The Arts Council, Dublin City Council, Siân Cunningham and all the staff at Dance House, John Cummins of Agtel, Sheila White, Gene Rooney, Gaiety School of Acting, Marty Rea, Aisling Mooney, Niamh O'Donnell and all the staff at Project, Amy Dawson, John McCormack, Bernadette Bohan, Pat Hargadon, Claire Shanahan, Fiona Moriarty, Debbie Maher and Nick Banyard, Jill Clark, Jane Curtin, Naomi Fitzgibbon, Spiff and all at doop design, Storytellers Theatre Co, Fishamble Theatre Co, 3G Phones Henry St Dublin, The George, Marks & Spencer Mary St Dublin, Carroll's Irish Gift Shop

## AND PARTICULAR THANKS TO OUR MAIN SPONSORS

**ACTION BREAST CANCER**
**(A Programme of the Irish Cancer Society)**

**AVON BREAST CANCER CRUSADE**

a programme of
irish cancer society

AVON
BREAST
CANCER
CRUSADE

### Corporate Patrons
John Cummins at Agtel, Coca Cola Bottlers Ireland, Novartis, Pembroke Capital Limited, Roche Pharmaceuticals

### Corporate Donors
Swords Laboratories, Elan

### Ribbon Tree Donors
Breda Cashe, Civic Theatre, Liam Meade, Eileen Meade, Gerard Ryan, Noirín Meade & Rory Costelloe, Pat Moylan, Anne Clarke, Ryan Meade & Susan Lawson, Donal Shiels, Lorraine Connolly, Eddie Tighe, Elaine Kennedy, David Wallace, Yvonne Ussher, Dawn Bradfield, Margaret Kelly, Margaret McGrath, Kieran Brennan, Suzanne Phelan, Megan Kelly, Barbara Eagar, Kate & Luke, Patrick Sutton, Caitlin & Meg P., Donna Geraghty, Mary & Colin, Katy Davis, Sean Kelly, Karen Ardiff, Judy Jetté, Jo Donohoe, Tom Ferris, Eamonn Kearns, Kieran O'Callaghan, Paula Furlong, Elayne Tighe, Simon O'Gorman, John & Petrina, Tony Kelly, Gary & Mary Burke

### Gúna Nua Friends
Liam & Eileen Meade, Mary & Michael Hennessy, Kathryn Raleigh & Colin D'Arcy, Aisling Meade & Cormac Gahan, Finola & David McKevitt, Breeda Clarkin, David & Caroline Hanly, Mary Jennings, Ann Hartnett, Brian Friel

### Special Thanks
Nestlé, Innocent Drinks, Brown Sugar, Column Fleming at The Clarence Hotel, The Tea Room at the Clarence, The Odeon Bar and Grill, Anne Roche at Roches Hair Solutions, Karen Jackson at Gardini

### Gúna Nua Board
Garry Burke (Chair); Sheila Campbell, Catherine Deane, Michael Hennessy, Marie Kelly, Brian Motherway, John Murray and Kathryn Raleigh

# UNRAVELLING THE RIBBON

Mary Kelly and Maureen White

*for*
*Mam, for the storytelling*
*M. K.*
*and*
*Ed, with love and thanks*
*M. W.*

## Characters

ROSE, *thirty-four, a hairdresser, lives in Tipperary on a farm with her husband Mike and her children Lyndsey and Malcolm*

LYNDSEY, *eleven, Rose's daughter*

LOLA, *in her fifties, lives in Dublin*

A forward slash in the text (/) marks the point where the next speaker interrupts.

*This text went to press before the end of rehearsals and may differ slightly from the play as performed.*

**Prologue**

*Dark. We hear a clapping rhythm. Spot fades up on* LYNDSEY *playing her clapping game. Spot fades out.*

*Light fades up on* LOLA, *stage right, and* ROSE, *stage left.*

LOLA. Definitely the waiting. Yes, the waiting . . .

LYNDSEY. Flying!

ROSE. Multi-tasking.

LOLA. Waiting for appointments, waiting for tests . . .

LYNDSEY. Being able to talk under water.

ROSE. Trusting my instincts, getting dressed up.

LOLA. Waiting for diagnosis, waiting for treatment . . .

LYNDSEY. And everything I touch turns to chocolate!

ROSE. Feeling beautiful – not just the clothes but my thoughts, my imagination.

LYNDSEY. And I'm not eleven I'm any age and I can go wherever I like.

ROSE. Feminine. Femininity . . . Hard to say exactly but I'd know if it was gone.

LOLA. Amazon women used to remove a breast in order to shoot their arrows with better accuracy.

**ACT ONE**

**Diagnosis**

*Lights up on the stage.* LYNDSEY *stops clapping and picks up an Argos catalogue.* ROSE *moves downstage left, faces audience, crosses arms.* LOLA *opens a real-estate brochure stage right.*

*Lights up on* ROSE *and* LYNDSEY.

ROSE, *distracted, arms crossed over breasts, looking out the window.*

LYNDSEY *reads from catalogue.*

LYNDSEY. 'Wave goodbye to frizz and get salon-perfect results every time with high performance straighteners to tame even the most unruly hair. Ceramic plates for high-gloss finish. Ten temperature settings. LCD display. Hanging loop. Handle lock. Auto shut-off. Three-metre cable. Heat resistant pouch. Even heat distribution technology. Two year guarantee.'

Please Mam?

ROSE. What?

LYNDSEY. Can I get a hair straightener?

ROSE. We'll see.

LYNDSEY. Well can I at least get a bra?

ROSE. When you need one.

ROSE *moves away from* LYNDSEY *to look out window again.*

LYNDSEY. When I need one . . . I did the breast test before dinner and NOTHING. Not a thing.

LYNDSEY *demonstrates the breast test, slapping the right side of her chest with her right hand and then the left side with her left hand. She shakes her head.*

Not a scrap of pain. I can't really tell yet which of my friends have passed the breast test but most of them tell me they have. Sophie, my best friend who never lies said she did the breast test last week and passed. I nearly died of disappointment because that would mean I'm the only one still failing. When I

4

pressed her further for details she said on the fifth slap she felt pain. I was so relieved. You only pass it if you cannot bear to slap after the second. Everyone feels pain on the fifth – even boys. I didn't say that to Sophie though. She gets things wrong in school all the time and she looks so sad when she realises. I never want Sophie to be sad. She has a lot to worry about though. Her cat Mildred has ignored her for three days now. Sophie's beside herself.

Everything about Sophie is perfect except she looks up to Tammy. I wish I had hair under my arms and then maybe I'd have Sophie all to myself. My life would be so simple if Tammy Flynn hadn't been born or if she has to be born then she doesn't have hair under her arms. Mammy doesn't listen to me – look, there she is staring out the window at the glasshouse. Probably watching Malcolm, her favourite child. He told me he heard on the news that some mushroom pickers have taken a likin' to bringing a few home in their pockets and he said, 'If there's thieves to be found I'll find them.' How immature can you get?

He probably goes there to fiddle with his testicles. Tammy Flynn only thinks he does it when she's around. He does it all the time. It's embarrassing enough without Tammy thinking she's the cause of it.

*Lights up on* LOLA.

*She closes the brochure and starts to arrange her space with the objects she'll unearth during the play. She's busy throughout this monologue.*

LOLA. Women my age can become invisible. When I finished chemo five years ago I planned to combat this. My husband and I didn't talk of my sick time after it was over, not even once. There has been massive disruption to insuring my visibility, but anniversary five brings a new hope and waking up in jail is a great sign.

I've been a campaigner for years and been thrown in a cell for much more worthy reasons. Yesterday I just lost my cool. I was in town framing one of my husband's paintings, and when I got back to my car an elderly man in a BMW was reversing into the space beside mine. I was standing at the passenger door of my car strapping in the painting when he slapped my ass. He had reversed in, reached from his open window and helped himself. So I snapped the BMW sign off his bonnet and keyed his car. I wasn't very co-operative when the guards arrived so off we went to jail.

When you're sick, all the things you can't do drive you berserk. I could never fully grasp why I hadn't done them when I was well. I promised myself when I had the energy and wherewithal, I'd get working on my list of things to do. Number one on my to-do list is to move out of this ridiculously large house. I was ready three years ago and then I couldn't face it; circumstances halted me. Moving involves sorting, picking up every single thing you own and examining its worth, allowing its smell, appearance or existence to unearth its story. Memories can kill you. I used to think they were more dangerous than cancer. If only we could ban them, find a cure. I tried smoking too much grass but that only affects short-term memory.

So, my bow and arrow is on the ready because on anniversary number five, on my return from prison, I put our house on the market.

ROSE. I found it this afternoon. A lump.

Finding is a funny word; it sort of suggests I was looking for something. Discovered is better or even it presented itself – sort of popped up to say 'hi!' Mam used to always say that I was trying to push me breasts down to me waist 'cause I always cross my arms above them. Glad now I didn't stop. I was standing at the kitchen window, hands folded over my chest. I was sort of glazing over, watching Mal holding fort at the glasshouses, wondering how long he'd last, sort of admiring his tenacity, I think I was watching his eight-year-old bold face ... thinking he didn't get the guts gene from me. I was only half-thinking thoughts though, glazing over the way you can with the countryside in front of you and then there she was – Lily.

I've named her already because it sounds little and I suppose I want to give her an identity, separate to mine. Somewhere in that daydream the palm of my right hand acknowledged her. Just like that, during a daydream at the kitchen window, Lily arrived.

Two useless things – leaning on your breasts and daydreamin' helped me find Lily.

Funny how I didn't move, just let thoughts come and go. I even thought of pretending it was five minutes ago and I never found it.

I don't want to admit this part but, just like Lily, it keeps presenting itself to me. Ya see, I had a thought, 'twas a quick one and certainly didn't last, it's been hauntin' me all evening though. 'Twas only a second, but I still had it, you know, it wasn't so much the thought as the feelin' that went with it ... The feelin' was ... excitement ... and the thought was ... maybe Mike will stand up and pay attention now.

I must have had tears in me eyes 'cause I remember them spillin' and tiny Malcolm down at the glasshouses came into focus again, little Mal full of defiance and I knew that only a real rotten mother would've had a thought like that.

LOLA (*sorting through belongings for the move, finds pink nail polish*). Ah, Jenny! I got this from Jenny, Archie's ex-P.A.

*She starts painting her nails with it and examining the results.*

Fashion – CASH IN! Seriously, girlie-women, women in pink? What is it all about? I like to call them mice. Pretty women with high-pitched voices, I've always wanted to choke them, and not because they are pretty and have high-pitched voices but because they tend to all dress the same – frilly girls, tiddlywinky girls. I'm sure there has to be a direct correlation between women who wobble along in ridiculously high heels and a low IQ. How can one follow fashion when different styles suit different types? Wrote an article about it one year in *Art Today*. They only printed it because of Archie's profile and you can be assured no mice read *Art Today*. Anyway, after my first bout of chemo I finally adopted my 'live and let live' policy. Still avoided mice but didn't feel the need to snap their spines when I was exposed. Chemotherapy helps one prioritise what one is going to let bother one.

Clothes that fit you, complement you, colours that are you. Orange makes me look ill. Will not wear, eat or look at the colour if I can help it. I adore white however.

Empire line, Victorian collars – any high necks now for my flat chest but never pink, never.

Jenny was a mouse, all squeaky and pink and cloney. One day Archie called out for her to come to the studio (I was upstairs so I could hear). He called her 'generic' by accident. I dropped the vase I was holding and nearly choked stifling a laugh and even though I was upstairs and couldn't see him, I knew that Archie blushed.

LYNDSEY. Sophie says if I want to be her best friend again I need to catch up. She wants to know if I've noticed that fashion has left me behind. I haven't. I don't even know what she means. I do know it sounds like something Tammy would say.

Being eleven is so complicated.

I told Sophie I hadn't noticed and would she help me catch up. 'Open your eyes,' she said and did a twirl. I still don't get it and I'm supposed to be the clever one.

At the end of next year we get to do a big project in two's on anything we want and we present it to the whole school. Last year two boys did it on Spies – it was so good. They even showed clips of *James Bond*. That's how I decided to be a private investigator. Sophie and I have agreed to do Australia because Daddy has loads of maps and things from Australia. Mammy and Daddy were going to go there a long time ago. They didn't but their friend Dessie went and stayed there and every Christmas he sends us gorgeous Australian things like a boomerang and a kangaroo with a baby one in the pouch. They're all on Daddy's Australia shelf but he's already agreed to lend them to us next year. Dessie even agreed to record a podcast describing Australia. I can't bear to think that Sophie might back out.

I was bursting to know if Mildred was still ignoring her but she'd gone to sit with Tammy so I went and sat beside the window in class and wished I was nine again.

ROSE. 'Doireann,' says I, 'I've to get a fuckin' biopsy.' And she rolled her eyes because I swore but then she revved up and kept saying, 'No GP would risk makin' a diagnosis, he's just being careful.'

I was glad she didn't ask why Mike hadn't come. My sister can be fair nosey. I just didn't want to say I hadn't told him.

I wanted to see the sea. Remind myself that everything keeps moving. Course, I said nothin'.

On the way home I just listened to the posh accent on Doireann, sorta soothing. Me father'd turn in his grave. She married a dentist from Cashel. After their first date she was posh – within hours, imagine, like magic. Me father didn't know what she was sayin' for weeks. And the dentist couldn't understand us. He's used of us now. You'd think with that bein' a quare start to a relationship it'd not bode well, but they're the best of friends, the two poshies, smilin' away at each other.

Lyndsey did the talkin' at dinner. I knew if it were a normal day I'd be sayin', 'No more guardin' the glasshouses after school, Mal.' It's been goin' on a week now, but I couldn't care less. Lyndsey was on a high, ate two full plates and didn't seem to be breathin' she spoke so fast. We heard all her news, from where she sees herself in twenty years (she's going to be a private investigator) to how a hair straightener is a necessity these days, Mike listened to every word. You can say a lot of things about Mike but he really listens to his children. I liked watching the big lump of a farmer considering the usefulness of a hair straightener.

I didn't listen like Mike did. I was sort of twenty miles away from everything. I just held me breath. Me and Lily were waitin' for the biopsy.

I did a lot of pretending I was listening to my children this week.

Mal kept me more than distracted by tryin' to put one of the Polish girls into handcuffs. She came up and knocked at the door. At first, she said, it was funny but then he wouldn't stop and then a stone hit her in the head. Mark, his pal, was hidin' in the bushes with the slingshot. I was mortified. Malcolm said she was stealin' mushrooms. I put him in his room for the day and drove Mark home. Mal's beside himself and Mike was only too happy to give me that look, the one that says, 'You handled that badly, Rose.'

LOLA *pulls out a bird costume, dusts it down, smells it. Starts sewing it.*

LOLA. My mother always said to me, 'No man will be able for you, Lola, tone it down.' Then Archie came upon me when he was out pheasant shooting. I was dressed like a bird and wore a sign saying, 'Would you shoot me?'

*To Archie as if he is in the room.*

I remember thinking how handsome you were and how boringly old school, I mean hunting. You couldn't tell me quick enough that you were an artist, as if that could forgive your murderous acts.

*To audience.*

But we sat in the long grass for hours and he really listened to me. He said he'd never hunt again. Then we made love, quite unorthodox really.

*She listens – Archie has corrected her.*

Okay, okay darling. It was unorthodox for Archie anyway.

I noticed the hair in his ears and he noticed me noticing it. He told me a joke about a snail to distract me. Ridiculous tactic and joke for that matter. Then asked if he could paint me and I said certainly – a much more sophisticated distraction.

I recalled my mother's words as I stood in that unnaturally uncomfortable position. 'Tone it down, Lola, no man will be able for you, tone it down.' Out of a certain rebellion against my mother and an uncontrollable urge to never leave his side, I proposed to him then and there. I was confident of a positive reaction since I had my assets on show.

He told me to not speak to him while he's working.

It was then I knew he was 'able for me'.

Fifteen minutes later he finished the painting and said 'yes'.

*As if Archie is in another room and she wants him to hear.*

One more minute and he would have been too late.

What am I going to do with this?

*Holds up bird costume.*

I can't just throw it out.

ROSE. 'Twas a week ago today that I got the biopsy and now we're waiting for the results, Doireann and me, side by side in a tiny waiting room. The receptionist just farted. I wanted to laugh. Doireann tut-tutted. Then I was more embarrassed by my sister than the receptionist was about her fart.

All the doctor had told me about the biopsy was that it'd be a 'fine-needle biopsy'. I acted like I knew what that meant. Why on earth didn't I just ask him? Suppose I was relieved it wasn't a fat needle. Then I met the biopsy doctor and realised I take out my new personality when dealing with doctors. I want them to like me, think I'm clever, brave and I don't want to take up much of their time. Maybe they'll give me good news if I have this personality. I'll be a good girl and then there won't be any trouble. I was in getting the biopsy last week, missin' my mother, remembered Doireann sitting outside in her funeral formalwear. I know she's missing Mam too.

They stuck the fine needle straight into Lily – ha ha stabbed in the heart, Lily. Oh, don't let anything seep out of her – is that possible? Of course I didn't ask. Some of Lily went into the syringe. She's made of skin and blood. Is that what cancer looks like? Didn't ask that either. A mammogram was thrown in for good measure. Me breasts haven't been crushed for a while. It reminded me of Johnny Brady squeezin' my breasts behind the sheds at the creamery – cold, hard and I'm not ready for this. It was like he wanted to take them home with him. I was afraid they'd burst Lily and she'd spread. Can that happen?

I rushed the kids this mornin' to be ready for school so I could drop them, and be back and ready for Doireann to pick me up for the results. Lyndsey told me in no uncertain terms that I was ruining her life, and Mal's still not speakin' to me over the attempted arrest scenario. I was so sorry to be rushin' them and startin' their day hassled. I hadn't really asked Mal what he was doin' down at the bloody glasshouses in the first place, and Lyndsey was getting that twisted look in her eye, that tormented-by-hormones look.

Maybe they'd both tried to explain and I'd only pretended to listen.

I'll make it up to them when I get the results and I can get on with things. I wish they'd call me for the results, I don't want to piss off the receptionist by asking how much longer. Doireann is still giving her a filthy look over the fart. Oh God, hurry up, please.

LYNDSEY. This has been the unluckiest day of my life so far and it's Tammy Flynn's fault. I kept a seat for Sophie today in art – we always sit together in art – and she pretended not to hear me callin' her when she came in with Tammy. They sat together at the table facin' mine in the art room and Sophie wouldn't look at me. Then Fergal Mooney sat beside me and he has germs. I am not doing my Australia project with Fergal Mooney.

And if that isn't enough for one day, we were at the stupid supermarket this evenin' and my Dad decides to stop and talk to Tammy Flynn's mother. I just stared at the potatoes like I didn't care. Then Tammy whispered my name, I looked up like a fool and she was scratchin' her cheek with her two fingers – her fuck-off fingers. She had a big grin on her face. I just ran. I made sure I had stopped cryin' by the time Daddy and Malcolm came out 'cause I knew Daddy would only be askin' me what was wrong. And what can he do about it? Nothin'!

ROSE. Not a word out of me. Not when he said 'do you understand' or 'are there any questions' or even when he said it was 'not all bad news'. All I did was grin like an eejit, wanting him to know I was polite in situations like this, smiling as if he was telling me something wonderful. I kept looking at his hands thinking how big and beautiful they were and of course didn't I need to think that. Isn't he going to be using those surgeons' hands on me next Friday.

Lily is cancer. The doctor says he'll take the breast and see about the lymph nodes. It seems there's more to Lily than meets the eye.

That's fine. Action I can take. It's waiting and not knowing that had me in knots for the last few days. Feel like I've woken up. We can do something about Lily now. Action stations.

Friday I'll have the operation . . . Next Friday . . . That's okay . . . Friday.

LOLA (*wrapping candleholders*). When I leave the house, I exit through the back door. When I enter it's the same way. On the odd occasion someone will call to the front door, and I will have terrible trouble navigating the boxes in the hall – but the real challenge is getting the door open as all the post blocks it shut. I've not only taken to ignoring post, I don't even pick it up. Every now and again circumstance will force me to deal with the guilt mountain wedging my door shut. I call it my guilt mountain as it is a pile of invites to exhibition openings – Archie's art friends. I never go, or reply, hence the guilt.

A young girl knocked on the door today looking for sponsorship for her school walk. She couldn't have been more than seven and very polite. Middle-class children usually bore me but this little lady seemed okay so I sponsored her and offered her some of my home-made fudge. She squeezed through the gap in the door and announced there was a smell in my house. The sterilised generation. On seeing that I store my fudge in a sock, she refused it. I was wrong about her and escorted her out. Then I set my guilt alight by having a bonfire of invites in the garden.

I did however hold onto one – Angela's. She's one of Archie's
more bearable friends so I've decided to attend her birthday
next month.

*Indicates candleholders she's wrapping.*

I have a gift now so I don't have to think about it again until
the night arrives. So many invites to so many occasions, you
have to go to something.

I got them in the antique shop. I got there via my front door
now that there's space again. I browsed, loving the smell of
old wood. There was a young woman behind the counter. She
couldn't stop smiling. Then her boyfriend came in and they
both couldn't stop smiling. I started earwigging when I heard
'Valentine's day'. Would she like to go for dinner and see a
movie on the day? She would. They kiss.

I spend all afternoon in there smelling old wood and spying on
young love.

ROSE. How the fuck do I tell the kids?

It's two o'clock and I'm pickin' them up at half two. I finished
at the doctors at 9.30 this morning and I'm hung over already.

Do I tell the kids?

They're eight and eleven, they know what cancer is.

Can I just not tell them, say it's something else?

Doireann's eyes were out on sticks when I got back to the
waitin' room this morning. I said nothing until we were in the
car.

I told her and she closed her eyes. Green eyeshadow on the lids,
seemed so stupid, imagine spending any time at all applying
green eyeshadow.

She opened her eyes and then her diary and pencilled in my
operation like it was a manicure. I wanted to smash her face in.
I didn't. She turned on the engine. I panicked.

Wait, Doireann, how do I tell the kids . . . and Mike?

She said I need to tell them all together. That way I only have
to say it once.

I asked her to drop me to the salon.

13

I caught Dave's eye through the window and pointed towards Roche's.

On my second vodka I told him.

He asked which one.

Fuck off, Dave, it's next Friday, I'm getting the whole lot removed.

He looked down – not like Doireann did or like Mike would in an embarrassed, useless way, but in a sad sort of a way.

I felt sorry for him. Why was I feeling sorry for him?

How do I tell the kids, Dave?

Apparently I should tell them the truth as their imaginations will do more damage otherwise.

We hugged for a long time.

What if I explain everything but I don't use the word 'cancer'?

Dave said the village is too small. They'll hear it somewhere.

Fuck! He's right.

He asked if he could have one last feel and I laughed for the first time today.

Thanks, Dave.

I walked home drunk, and fell asleep.

LYNDSEY. Mammy is going into hospital on Friday to get her left boob taken away because there are parts of it that will make her sick if she doesn't. That means that I'll have to spend the weekend with boring Malcolm when Daddy's working.

Just when I thought my life couldn't get any worse.

LOLA *finds a brass cat, puts it aside, then another and then another.*

LOLA. Memories can kill, so sometimes you've to not deal with certain memory makers. Discard them quickly, out of sight in order to put the brakes on the memory. Press pause so it doesn't play itself. This trick proves difficult, impossible in fact, when there are thirty-seven memory makers for the memory you're avoiding. Where's my bow and arrow?

*She holds a brass cat and closes her eyes.*

It's the feel of it.

When I was sick, Archie got me a gift for every treatment. Paintings at first then the smell of oil paints got too much. Comedy worked for a while, but then . . . not anymore. Sometimes we'd lie down for the evening, side by side. After a while we did that a lot. It was all I was able for. He loved doing that. He loved being near me. I did it for him. I felt so radioactive and disgusting. I was furious. He was never afraid of my anger. Everyone was afraid of my anger but he loved it. 'So spirited, so alive', he'd say.

*To Archie.*

You used to say you were useless. Didn't know what to do to protect me. Sadness can be contagious, and no one asked how you were. I hadn't the energy.

Then you saw the first cat. It was in the window of Knobs and Knockers and it was crying out to be bought. Brass and dignified and Egyptian with a scarab around its neck, like it was guarding the gates to the underworld.

*To audience.*

He bought me one for every day of chemo and every day of radiation. And then when the cancer came back and took my right breast he bought me more cats.

*To Archie.*

'Lost Lanes', my favourite painting, went missing around that time. You better not have sold it to fund my gifts. I loved that painting. I better find it when going through the attic, Archie.

He did great menus – dairy-free, his research told him. I trusted his menus. Handwritten, I'd study them closely. Held them close to my eyes. I refuse to wear glasses and he'd wait, wait to hear my order. He loved that too.

*To Archie.*

You missed my voice. I pretty much stopped talking. You'd find ways to make me speak – animals were the key. I laughed at our neighbour's dog, told him he was mischievous. I spoke. You cherished that. The smells from your studio got too much so you moved it, stopped going to it. We lay down beside each other a lot then, always in the dark, curtains pulled. Thirty-seven cats in total.

*The following scene won't be played naturalistically; it will be played with* ROSE *and* LYNDSEY *each in their own space.*

ROSE. I'll be in and out before you know it . . .

LYNDSEY *still crying.*

Is it the hair? We don't even know that I'm definitely getting chemotherapy, and if I do I'll get a wig, Lynd, Doireann will be here every week and Mike . . .

LYNDSEY (*coming up for air*). What's wrong with you?

Does it always HAVE to be about YOU? (*Mimics her.*) 'I'm sick, I've to go to hospital.'

Well at least you have friends . . .

LYNDSEY *starts bawling again,* ROSE *relieved it's about friends.*

ROSE. What's going on?

LYNDSEY (*mimics her*). 'What's going on?' Do I actually have to tell you to be interested in my life?

ROSE. Lyndsey, cut it out, what's going on?

LYNDSEY. Great, now you hate me too . . .

ROSE. I don't . . . (*Softer.*) What is it?

LYNDSEY. Basically my life is over. Tammy and Sophie are best friends now and Tammy has her period and even uses tampons and she said I'm a boy.

*Cries again.*

She gave me the F-off fingers in the supermarket.

ROSE. That's awful.

LYNDSEY. I know.

*Starts bawling again.*

*Then runs out of tears.*

ROSE. Do you want me to go and . . .

LYNDSEY. No!

ROSE. Okay then, goodnight.

LYNDSEY. 'Night.

*Pause.*

Mam?

ROSE. Yeah?

LYNDSEY. Malcolm thinks cancer is green.

*They laugh.*

ROSE *leaves.*

LYNDSEY (*scared*). Is it contagious?

*Looks up and* ROSE *is gone.*

ROSE. Mike's only concern is the kids. He didn't ask me when it started, how I found the lump, how did I feel? Why I hadn't told him sooner? He didn't come near me. He sort of slouched against the door staring at the kids' faces and waited for it to be over.

I wish my mother was still alive.

Lyndsey Googles a word a night on Mike's computer and he oversees it. She told me this evening that she Googled 'private investigator'. Between that and the bullying, she really can't be all that concerned about me. Mal just acted like I was depriving him of *The Simpsons*, as it took longer than the ad break to explain. I'm so relieved.

What will I look like? I'll 'probably need chemo due to the size of the tumour'. I hope my moustache falls out and my leg hair. They may take some lymph nodes. They'll know for sure when they open me up. Creepy. Thank God they knock you out for this sort of stuff.

I can't really imagine the chemotherapy or what I'll look like without hair or a breast but I know, not like a passing thought, I can just really feel that my body is never goin' to be the same again. All the efforts to cover up, hide the stretch marks and to buy the right bra, the one that gives you cleavage, the hair-styles, the hair dye, the hair straighteners, conditioners, curlers, the fake tan, all the rituals, ridiculous, so ridiculous. God I'd love to be ridiculous again.

I want chemotherapy though. I want it zapped outta me. I keep thinkin' of the computer game Mal plays, *Minesweeper*, obliterate Lily and all her friends.

When Doireann rang this afternoon to see how I am, I cried
'cause she sounded like she really wanted to know the answer.
Then there was that excruciating silence when Doireann
doesn't know what to do or say. I immediately regretted it.

Finally I heard an almost inaudible, 'Now, now', and I'm quite
sure, just for a moment, a tiny second, I heard her Tipperary
accent.

LOLA. I would love to be a heavy drinker, turn to the bottle of
whiskey at times like this. Not having anywhere to put your
anger is torture. I used up a certain amount on pig-man – my
real-estate agent – but he was gone too quickly to let me
drain it away. Now I'm here with it, I don't particularly enjoy
getting drunk, and going for a long walk just feels too
positive right now.

The little pup. I'm at least twice his age. His stupid squashed
ignorant face all tanned with spiky greasy hair on top.

'Your home is in no fit state for viewing. It needs a massive
clear-out and a spring clean if we're to get a fair price for it.'

That's what I'm in the process of doing, imbecile.

It's not quick and it's not easy.

Idiot!

That's it. I'm bringing my business elsewhere.

LYNDSEY. The night of Mammy's operation Doireann took us
to Roche's for dinner. It was ridiculous. We spent the entire
time talking about Malcolm wanting to be an astronaut. Why?
We know he won't be. When he was six he wanted to be an
Alsatian. We had to talk about that too.

Why are we out for dinner and Mammy is in the hospital?
What's the point of me passing the breast test if I'll have to get
them cut off like Mammy?

Malcolm is at his testicles again. Maybe we could get them cut
off.

ROSE. I read five *Hello!* magazines waiting to be checked in. An
interview with Olivia Newton John and a woman who said she
got reconstructive surgery and they looked amazing. What
does that mean? Does amazing mean they look like breasts or
they look like they used to or is it just amazing that you have
more than a flat scar?

Then there's Kylie, looking fantastic, as good as ever. I wonder what she got done.

Imagine being far on enough to be able to think about getting reconstructive surgery. The luxury of caring what I look like again. Actually choosing to have another operation. I'd want my stretch marks and my droopy breast back.

Dr Mills said that a woman called Ellen will fit me for my prosthesis after surgery. I can't bear it. What if I can't look at myself? I've to be fitted for a pretend breast. Who's that for? It might look even and balanced, but how will I feel even and balanced? More *OK!* magazine.

Mike is outside feeding the parking meter. There was a time when he knew my breasts better than I did.

Doireann is beside me. She's reading *Pride and Prejudice*.

LOLA. I put my thirty-seven cats around the front door. I'd like to know what the real-estate pup would think of that. It's partially to protect me from the likes of him and toffee-nosed middle-class children, but it's also because I think the shadow is back. Haven't seen it for ages but today just coming to the front door I saw it out of the corner of my eye, waiting for me to see it before it disappeared.

Feel like things are shifting, going backwards, no mark's being made around here.

*During the following,* ROSE *is a bit drugged – just waking up from the operation.*

ROSE. The last thing I remember is Doireann telling me to be sure they get the right one, she knew a man once who lost his right leg when . . .

Mike looming over me . . . Elongated and echoey voice . . . Try to smile.

It is Mike, isn't it?

He seems very tall.

Isn't morphine lovely . . .

My lovely morphine, is everything my morphine dream or is some of it real?

Who cares?

Mike looming again.

I wish he could see himself.

What's he saying?

Doesn't matter, I am very busy dancing at Lyndsey's wedding.

Clear now, no drugs in the way, very clear and bargaining like a pro – just let me live till Lyndsey's wedding . . .

Morphine.

Mike backing away.

Arm heavy.

Drains at my side.

Where are the  . . .

Are these bandages  . . .

Is my breast  . . .

Sleep.

LYNDSEY. Mammy was still in bed when I got up this morning. I hope she's okay. She has a big long bandage down her arm because I think they removed some of that too. She only has one breast now. I have none and she has one. What sort of family are we at all? I hope Sophie and Tammy don't find out.

*End of Act One.*

## ACT TWO

### Treatment

ROSE. Six months of chemotherapy, every third Monday, five weeks of radiation daily, five minutes per day. The type of chemotherapy drugs that do cause hair loss, fatigue and possibly nausea, but anti-nausea drugs are supplied. Chemo starts in a month. Give me a chance to 'bounce back' from the operation.

Was told all this the day after my operation and couldn't recall one word of it when Mike and Doireann came in. Doireann got very annoyed so Mike got very quiet. When Doireann stormed off to get information, Mike put his hand on my forehead. That felt really good. I closed my eyes and we both ignored the bandage covering my no breast. Doireann found Dr Mills, updated herself, came back and announced my treatment plan to us. Then she returned to *Pride and Prejudice*. She could have left us alone. After an incredibly empty silence, Mike announced he'd milkin' to do. Doireann rolled her eyes. He left. Milkin' . . . udders . . . breasts. Fuck!

Doireann's been rattling off my treatment plan and symptoms ever since, like it's a song she heard on the radio. Every time I see her she says it to me. There's even a rhythm to it. It has completely lost all meaning. She has Mal saying it now like a rap.

LYNDSEY. Mam's first day of chemo today. I made Malcolm's poached egg. Why can't he just have cereal? Mammy noticed I was helping and kissed my head. I wonder if Mammy will still want to drop us to school when she has no hair. I'll say that I'll walk Malcolm there and back; she'll think I'm doing it to help.

ROSE. Dr Doireann drove me to Cork this morning. Day one of chemo. A month to the day since surgery. An hour's drive there and back every third Monday with Doireann.

Dr Mills had warned me that they'll take some blood when I get there and if my bloods are 'right' (didn't ask him what that meant), my Lily-specific concoction will be mixed and pumped into me.

Said a prayer for the first time since my confirmation – let my bloods be right, please. Time to start nuking Lily. The last month has been waiting hell; I've been going around with bits of Lily still in me, doing nothing about it. Doing nothing in general actually. My arm's too sore to wash my own hair let alone anyone's at the salon, and Mike has taken over the cooking so I've played hundreds of games of *Minesweeper*.

This morning when I heard that my bloods were right, I hugged Doireann. She was disgusted, mortified. She'll be on the alert for such attacks in future.

I followed Elaine, the nurse who looks Lyndsey's age, down the corridor. Don't start thinking about Lyndsey now.

I followed her into a ward. I counted twelve other women in the room, they all had a line into their hand. There was something familiar. I followed Elaine down the centre of the room. They all watched me. Do they know I'm new? First day at school. Their chairs lean back a bit and then I realise what's familiar – it's like the salon. They're getting their roots done. Elaine pointed out my leanie-back chair and the women started talking to each other, chattin'. They must have stopped when I came in. They're talking about spending S.S.I.A's. It's the chemo salon. When I sat onto my chair I saw the 'Poison' and 'Toxic' signs and behind them the women's mixtures, hanging on their drip stands, pumpin' into their bloodstreams.

I'm the youngest. The woman straight across from me was still looking at me. She was sorry I'm so young. She had an expression my mother would have. I grabbed a magazine before she talked to me. She gives me a lump in my throat. Don't look at lady who reminds me of Mam and don't think about Lyndsey. I'm going into battle. I need to be strong.

Elaine tells me the anti-nausea drugs will go in first. I swallow them. Bring it on. Another nurse arrived with my Lily-nuker, specifically designed to destroy Lily. It too has a sign saying 'Poison' and 'Toxic'. All the nurses wear gloves so they don't come in contact with it. Elaine put a line into my hand and I willed the stuff into me. I felt sick for a minute and then nothing. Relief maybe. Finally I'm doing something about Lily. I looked up at me mother across the way. She was still watching me. I stuck my magazine in front of my face.

From the safety of my magazine I started to realise where I was. I can't believe people have been going to these chemo salons for years. I never pictured it. I just never thought about how some people are spending their every third Monday.

LYNDSEY. I passed the breast test!

It was so sore. You can't see anything yet but they're on their way. At least something is working out. I can't tell Sophie the good news or anyone on the basketball team because I've been telling them I've passed it for the last three months. Slap number one and I roared with the pain. Malcolm stuck his stupid head round the door and I threw a shoe at him. Then I cried 'cause today Mam is too weak to listen to my complaints about him. She just sighs and turns over.

I went to Sophie's house to play with Mildred. Sophie wasn't there but I talked to Mrs Gallagher. I asked her if she'd bring me bra shopping when she's bringing Sophie. She didn't answer me. I went bright red. She sent me home with a cooked ham. I put it in our thorn bush.

ROSE. My second round of chemo tomorrow and word has spread. I knew it would through Dave at the salon but not this much. I counted forty-two cards today. They're a matter of course now. Eight were mass cards. I thought I'd died when I got the first one. In fairness though, I can't believe some of the people who've sent cards. The kids' principal never salutes me. If we have to deal with each other she doesn't look me in the eye. I got me first card from her. Then there's the people who ye just don't really know, a friend of a friend. I like that they made the effort. I wonder who told them.

My blood count has been okay so far. I can't get over the chatting. It's more like the salon every time. A lot of the women chat about ordinary, normal stuff. I don't, can't yet. But I have taken to listening in on their conversations while getting the Lily-nuker. It's amazing what can become normal. Dr Mills visits sometimes and I always grin at him like an eejit. Maybe if he likes me, Lily will disappear. I worry that I'm in love with him at times. He's so comfortable talking about cancer and my breast that it makes me feel important. I don't always listen to him – sometimes I just look at his face when he's talking. I wonder if he'd fancy a woman with one breast? He started talkin' about my fertility today. He's so concerned with how I'm feeling that I want to propose to him. Early onset of menopause is a possibility – not listening – no more children – not listening – how do I feel? Swallowin' that lump in my throat was not far off the challenge of childbirth. Can't cry in front of Dr Mills or my mother across the way because I'll never stop.

LYNDSEY. I've actually started playing with Malcolm. There is nothing to do around here except for jobs. Mammy is no fun and I know that nobody is any fun when they're sick but most people are only sick for a week. Doireann isn't very good at maths so she's not really helping me with my homework. I wish everything could go back to the way it was when Sophie was my best friend and Mammy could do more than just play board games.

I Googled 'cures for boredom' last night and Daddy laughed. I'm glad he thinks it's funny but it wasn't supposed to be. Then he told me he wanted to e-mail Dessie in private. I hate when he does that. I ended up playing hide-and-seek with Mal. He always hides in the same place. I'm never having children.

ROSE. I'm losing hair and it makes me feel sicker than the chemo. I make sure it's all off the pillow before Mike wakes up. If nobody else sees it then it's not happening. So I've taken to peering over the top of my magazine and spying on the wigs and choices of headscarf. Nora has a beautiful, blondie-grey wig. She's in her late sixties so she's incorporated the grey. It's really well styled and I'm glad because I heard her tell me mother across the way that her husband insists that she wears it around the house. Asshole. I decided on headscarf myself when Doireann brought me pictures of an eight-hundred Euro red wig that's the exact same style and colour as her own hair. She wanted to buy it for me. I had to say something so I told her I decided on a headscarf, 'twas just a knee-jerk reaction to get her off my back. The women in the chemo salon have gorgeous wigs, so real and flattering.

I wonder if Doireann would be hurt if I started trying on some.

The nurses are like friends. I'm silent and they make up for it. When I leave I have that same feeling I did when I took Lyndsey home from the hospital – I can't believe they aren't coming home with me.

Dr Mills says the chemo has fully worked itself through my body ten days after I get it, and that's why I sleep all day and feel shit and even then there's a relief. Feels like it's working.

Am I going to die? Everyone says I won't but the fuckin' mass cards aren't helpin'.

LOLA. I no longer feel like an Amazonian warrior. I took the house off the market six weeks ago after that cheeky pup left and I haven't brought my business elsewhere because there is still so much to clear. It is time-consuming but only because some days I cannot face it. I found Archie's old laptop and pressed pause instantly. That's been put aside for another day. I'm more invisible than ever, and I'm not moving quickly, it's taking forever.

Clearing is exhausting. It's always bookended by a walk along Sandymount Strand – see the dogs. But dog walkers are killing two birds with the one stone these days – exercise and dog walk. They strolled and now they stride, less willing to let me speak to their dogs. It's worth a try, however, and ever so nice to get away from the piles of decisions lurking in every corner of our house waiting to be made.

I say I'm afraid of nothing, but when it gets down to the nitty-gritty, deciding what to do with everything down to a shopping receipt, I'm terrified.

Am I going to drown in this house?

It's Friday tomorrow I will go and visit the horses.

ROSE. Doireann calls Ronan, her husband, 'the hubby'. I can actually hear Mike's jaw tighten when she says it around him.

Doireann told me about Mona today on the way to Chemo. Mona is the hubby's assistant – his dental nurse. She's the one who owns the lime-green Beetle, my landmark for finding the practice. Mona is 'off sick' with breast cancer. She has been off sick for six months. Just finished treatment. She has three little boys – three Malcolms and a lime-green Beetle.

'Just finished treatment and she's doing okay.' What does that mean? Doireann will ask the hubby for more information. My jaw tightens.

More hair on the pillow this morning when I woke up. Didn't have the energy to remove it before Mike woke up. I felt him notice. He held his breath for what seemed like ages and then put his arm around me. I lay there stiff as a board and pretended to be asleep. It's not that easy, Mike.

*Beat.*

This afternoon he said, 'Come to the haybarn and I'll shave your head.'

I think he was trying but I am too tired to notice.

I said okay.

LYNDSEY. Mammy is a deadly hairdresser so when she told me Daddy was going to shave her head I couldn't believe it. Why didn't she ask Dave from the salon? What was she thinking?

I did my best to watch but Malcolm kept on burping and anyways did anyone even bother to ask how I felt about having a bald mother? No.

So I left. I heard Mam saying, 'Leave her be, Mike.' I wish she'd leave me be. Anyway what she doesn't know is that I got a hair straightener yesterday after school in the chemist with my own money. I keep it under the bed. I've burned my ears twice but I love it.

LYNDSEY *starts straightening her hair.*

*Sound of razor.*

ROSE *appears behind* LYNDSEY, *watching her. Just watching – then turns away.*

LOLA. I saw my horses today. I walk up to the riding school. It's only two miles away. I speak to them over the fence. I've named them all. I bring some apples. Floozy was delighted to see me today and I her, and after she'd eaten her apple she galloped across the field towards Dancer – her current boyfriend. The rhythm of her gallop, strong legs pounding, pulsating with force and elegance towards her man. What a wonderful tart you are, Floozy, a beautiful majestic tart.

LYNDSEY. We never go anywhere anymore. Life is totally boring. In fact I even find school interesting which just shows you exactly how exciting things are around here. Malcolm got in trouble again today. I heard Daddy and Mammy talking about it. It seems my eejit of a brother nearly got trampled to death. He was at the front of the cows and they started running and the only reason he didn't get trampled was he was in the middle of a daydream so he stayed still. Daddy's been telling us since we were babies to stand still if they start running so what I don't get is why Daddy hates it when Malcolm daydreams. He said 'He's just like you, Rose,' to Mammy and then they just stared at each other and Mal was outside lookin' in the window like a fool. I'd be scared too though especially 'cause I think Daddy was crying.

I hope Mammy's eyebrows will come back soon. I can't wait. I hate walking Malcolm to and from school.

ROSE. My sleep is all over the place. Watching *Oprah* at three a.m. Mike pretends to be asleep sometimes when I come to bed. Sleep is a funny thing. When he's actually asleep there is no tension in the room and when he's pretendin' you could cut it with a knife.

I'm glad our patterns are out of sync though, 'cause we haven't had sex since the operation and I hate pushin' him away. It's not that I'm ashamed or anything it's just we haven't even talked about my body changing. We haven't talked about anything. I was playing Joker Rummy with Lyndsey today and I'm convinced she was letting me win.

She's slippin' away from me and I can't get a grip of her.

So glad the kids have broken Doireann in. She used to pretend they didn't exist. Not in a cruel way – she just wasn't able for the muck and uncertainty of them. Lyndsey's killed complimentin' her clothes and Mal walks her to her car when she's leavin'.

After she left tonight Mal and I were playin' draughts. His hands scare me – they're like old friends. Mesmerisingly cute. They scare me because they're definitely something I cannot be without.

LOLA *is standing upstage facing the audience, there is an upstage window behind her. She is wearing a man's robe, she smells it.*

LOLA. Why are you still here?

You said I always distracted myself with surprising projects. When I was campaigning we had sex every chance we got – you loved my passion. I hope to campaign again soon, Arch, and not just against presumptuous BMW drivers. This move is just taking longer than I thought.

When I got sick the first time you said you 'missed the lunacy – nothing is worse than somebody giving up'. When breast number two was taken we lay down a lot together, in the dark of course. This body you knew so well, the body you made love to, painted, adored, this body would lie beside you but you were forbidden to see it now, curtains pulled. I wanted better for you, Archie. Wanted you to find someone who was complete, with big breasts who was energetic and passionate and able to love you. When you're sick for so long you can't imagine ever being well.

ROSE (*holding a mug*). The hubby said that Mona's hair's coming back. I'm getting obsessed with her. I can see her giving me mouthwash. I've more of a smell than a picture of her though – dentist's smell! But she's like a big sister to me now, one step ahead of me, doing everything first.

Last night I cried myself to sleep for Mona and her three little Malcolms. It's easier to cry for Mona.

LOLA. Do you remember the night during the dark time you came into the room at midnight, moonlight flooded the room. I didn't move, didn't cover up.

*Moonlight comes through window.* LOLA *turns and looks out the upstage window, she lets the robe hang open once her back is turned.*

*She looks to her right as if Archie is there.*

It's okay.

You didn't speak. I was searching your eyes; you were just so relieved you could see me again.

*Moonlit state fades.* LOLA *turns with robe wrapped around her again.*

Not long after that you said, 'I do miss them, and not in the way you'd think. They were there and part of us and then gone, that's all.'

ROSE *drops mug.*

ROSE. Shit, shit, shit.

*She starts cleaning it up.*

Mike asked me what's wrong.

WHAT'S WRONG? What's wrong is that I have no hair, Mike. What's wrong is that I'm too tired to brush my teeth.

Everything tastes like metal. I don't even know what Malcolm took in his lunch today. I hate the clothes Doireann bought for me. And now I've broken Lyndsey's fuckin' favourite mug – the one with the stupid horse in the red hat. She'll go mad! Mary Gallagher rang this afternoon and told me Lyndsey asked her to bring her bra shopping; she actually offered to do it, my little girl's first bra.

Do you know what I've done every morning for the last week? When I wake up? I force myself into the future with the kids, Mike. Lyndsey's debs and I'm there. Mal's graduation and I'm there. Weddings, leaving cert results, and I can't stop; I'm doing it all day. It's like a fucking addiction. I'm afraid if I don't do it . . .

What's wrong is I have no one to talk to.

He said I have him.

I said nothing.

*She returns to picking up the pieces.*

No, I don't have you, Mike. You didn't say one word when I told you. And you haven't said anything since.

*As if Mike has tried to help her.*

No! I can manage myself.

LYNDSEY. Yesterday Sinead O'Gorman shoplifted an ice-pink nail polish from Value Save. And she got caught. Tammy says she'll probably have to go to a detention centre in Cork. And this morning Mammy told me she'd broken my horse cup. Daddy eye-balled me as if to say, 'Don't complain.' You can't say anything in this house anymore.

Dessie rang Daddy today from Melbourne and outta practice for bein' a private investigator I listened at the door. I wish I hadn't now. Daddy said that he does most of the cookin' since Mammy's been sick and the housework and he covers if Doireann can't look after us and he takes the post before Mammy sees it and pays the bills and he has stopped half the village from callin' into her. I know that sounds okay but he was sayin' it really angry, like it was Mammy's fault. Then he said she thinks he does nothin' and she won't talk to him. Mammy's always saying things to Daddy. She never ignores

anyone. I said I couldn't think of a word to Google before bed
because I don't want to be near him. I think he's just mean.
Mammy's so tired I'm glad she didn't hear any of that. I hope
Dessie told him off. What's wrong with half the village callin'
to the house anyway? It might make it less boring around here.

I wish I could go to a detention centre in Cork.

LOLA *is unwrapping the painting that Archie brought on, she
looks at it, is deciding where to hang it, maybe dusts it off first.*

LOLA. Why is this hidden away?

*Turns it towards her.*

Oh, Jesus, you bought it back.

*Examines it.*

No matter how abstract, I can read your paintings like an expla-
nation is written in block capitals across the centre of them.

There have been times when you asked me to explain them to
you. Sometimes I'd make it up, I wasn't always sure you'd
want to know.

You painted so little when I was sick, but you painted some.
We paid little attention to who bought them.

Once the curtains were opened we started going out for dinner.

I was still quiet. You were so careful not to push me but you
were gently leading me back into the world.

I ordered fish mostly. I'd thank the fish for his life and then dig
in. I knew you were delighted I'd spoken. One evening after
I'd thanked the mackerel I met your eyes and they danced,
then in a low whisper you said 'flashes of my wife'. You were
holding your breath for moments like that.

Then there was the Seaview restaurant night.

Our favourite, well my favourite – sea bass!

That's when I saw this.

*She looks at the painting she's holding.*

I knew it was yours instantly. At first I was simply surprised that
the restaurant had purchased such a dark and erratic piece. Then
I really saw it. I read it. You were so alone, crushed and it was
my fault. I could see your struggle. I hated myself. You knew

what I was thinking. I left the restaurant and pulled the curtains again. You came to our room and told me that you didn't always feel that bad. I asked you not to lie with me again.

I stopped talking again, to you and the fish.

I thought that would do it, Archie. I really believed you'd go then because I had never before shut you out.

You went fishing every day then, brought home what you caught and cooked it for me. You were probably afraid to paint. I'd hear you thank each creature for its life as you placed my food inside the door. Where did you eat? Your room became the spare with the ridiculous four-poster bed. I had shut you out completely that time.

ROSE. I've lived all my life in the country and now it's too quiet. Nothing is happening. When I do get out I hate that everyone drops their eyes to my chest, trying to figure out which one's gone. When I was in McDaid's one of the Foley girls came in and looked like she'd seen a ghost when she saw me, then she asked in that 'oh dear you look dreadful' kind of voice, 'Are you all right?' I told her I was fine and that her roots need seein' to. Dave will be impressed – losing business and I'm not even at work.

I was spared anymore chit-chat because Johnny Brady's wife Kathleen came in and had a full-blown fit about stale bread they sold her. It didn't matter what it was about, it was a full-blown fuss. How I would love to have the energy to do that. How I would love to have the energy to give a shit about stale bread.

LOLA *takes out laptop. Places it on her knee, two hands face down on top of it.*

LOLA. You did give up a little bit in that four-poster bed. Nobody would ever have known if you hadn't told Angela. She told me when I was well that you had gotten really depressed in that spare room. I've never said that out loud before.

Archie always said that I made him believe in an afterlife, and he'd say, 'It's not because you're religious or even because you believe in an afterlife, but because you've a spirit that I can't imagine being contained by a burial or ended or eliminated in any way.'

Not sure that was always meant as a compliment.

31

*Silence,* LOLA *slowly opens the laptop.*

Each night before you'd retire to the spare room, you'd plug in your laptop outside my room – our room – you'd plug it in on the landing and play some of my favourite songs.

You'd announce that, 'DJ Banister', had arrived.

You even managed to sit through Dolly Parton one evening. I'd say that nearly killed you.

I'd fall asleep and you'd retire to the four-poster bed.

Angela told me, Archie.

She quoted you.

You said, 'I lay awake in the four-poster bed for two months coming to terms with the fact that my wife's spirit had indeed been eliminated.'

*She drops the laptop or slams it down.*

LYNDSEY. Can we go to Tramore?

LOLA (*moving quickly, frenetic, packing away belongings*). If this house doesn't sell soon I'm getting someone in. Some people keep students from abroad. An Italian student learning English, an Italian stallion in his thirties. It's okay. I know you'd hate that. There are so many empty rooms – why did we buy a place so big for two people?

LYNDSEY. Mam, can we go to a movie?

LOLA. I keep finding more of your black abstract stuff, Archie, the experimental stuff – I don't get them. I'm putting them in storage.

LYNDSEY. Dad, can we go camping again near Galway?

LOLA. Where is 'Lost Lanes'? Archie, your mother painted that. Tell me you didn't sell it.

LYNDSEY. I wish we could go to Fota Wildlife Park.

LOLA. I'm starting to notice the difference between the black abstract paintings. I think they tell a story. I'm guessing the order they should be viewed in. This is fucking torture. I think that one is your face, Archie. So sorry I didn't notice before. I need to get out.

LYNDSEY. Hurray! We are finally going somewhere – Dublin!

Shoppin' all day with Mammy. Mal and Doireann are coming too but really me and Mammy are the ones who love shopping. We haven't done this in ages. I figure we should go to Zara and HMV and Penneys and then to Claire's for accessories. They have gorgeous belts there. Of course it won't be all for me. Mam really needs some new clothes too. Her idea of getting dressed up these days seems to be anything with black track suit bottoms. 'Don't worry,' I told her 'I can give you expert advice.' I was even thinking this week I might go into fashion design but I'm not really a great drawer. Maybe I could be a partner with someone and I could have the ideas and they could do the drawings. Anyways I can't wait. Me and Mammy. Shoppin'!

ROSE. Oh Jesus, we're going shopping.

I asked Lyndsey if she asked Sophie's mum to take her bra shopping.

LYNDSEY. I didn't want to bother you . . . Is that okay?

ROSE. Of course. Go get ready.

LOLA. I give up. The more things I pull out to sort, the more untidy and unmanageable this place is. I can't get into the hall anymore let alone through the front door, and they'll cut off my electricity if I don't find and pay those bills.

ROSE. Doireann arrives dressed like she's goin' to a wedding. She's actually wearin' one of those standie-up flowers on her head. Lyndsey's impressed. I'm a bit frightened of it. Mal wraps himself around her. I can't believe me eyes.

Apart from an itchy wig, the car journey is hilarious. Mal produces an assortment of weapons he'll use if any of us are mugged, and Lyndsey has Doireann singin' those songs where the lyrics sound like curse words.

But when we get there and Doireann announces Brown Thomas, I know what I have to do. I took her aside and told her I just want to see the sea. She looked like she might cry, maybe because she thought she'd never get me dressed proper. But she nodded and drove me to Portmarnock and I looked out over the sea to thousands of miles away.

LYNDSEY. We were a stone's throw away from the turn for the car park near Claire's Accessories when Doireann announced we were goin' to the sea. I couldn't believe it. I just ignored them all. When we got there Malcolm asked if we could take the kites from the boot and fly them. Of course the answer was yes just because he is cute. I wish someone would tell me what's so cute about the smell of sweat and black toenails. It's so obvious Doireann prefers him. I stayed in the car.

ROSE. I only know when I'm lookin' over the sea that I fuckin' hate radiation. For me it's the worst part. First I got my tattoos – literally branded for life – four black spots where the radiation goes in. I've a dressing on 'cause the last session burnt my skin. I fuckin' hate it. It's twenty-five sessions, only a few minutes each but I can't stand goin' underground. Everyone leaves you there alone, while they run for cover. At least with chemo the nurses stay, even if they are wearing gloves. What am I supposed to think when everyone leaves the fuckin' room? Lying there in the basement.

The waves are folding in on themselves one after another tryin' to remind me that things move on. Well, sickness certainly does.

LYNDSEY. 'Twas only when Mammy wandered off down the beach on her own that I reached my limit. I don't remember anyone askin' me if I wanted to go to a stupid beach and then me mother who we're supposed to be spending the day with wanders off. I had my ten Euro from Daddy and my Claire's voucher. I know they'll probably catch up with me and try to make me come back but I won't. They've gone too far this time. So I'm going shopping on me own and now they'll be sorry I don't have a mobile like every single other person in my class (except Fergal Mooney). I just don't care.

LOLA. I needed a change of scenery although the scenery isn't much different here. I'm striding instead of strolling. I avoid making eye contact with anyone, even people with dogs. Tired of the dismissive looks from dog walkers and the suspicious looks from the instructors at the riding school, sick of people and their tiny minds. I lost 'Lost Lanes'. I always said if I'd a daughter I'd pass it onto her.

ROSE. When we got back to the car she wasn't there. That's all I know, Mike.

She's wearing her light blue jacket and jeans.

She's only eleven. Mike, what if someone took her?

*The following overlaps with* ROSE *down to* ROSE's *line:'Oh God I wish you were here'.*

LYNDSEY. I thought I knew the way but after walking for ages I couldn't see any shops just apartments and buildings and it didn't seem at all like a city centre. My heels were rubbing. Mam was right I shouldn't have worn my new white flat shoes but I just wanted everything to be perfect and now it was all wrecked. I keep on walking but it's starting to get dark and what if someone starts following me?

*She starts to cry.*

Mammy, I wish you were here.

LYNDSEY *runs off stage.*

ROSE. I'll fuckin' kill ya when I find ya, Lyndsey.

How do you know someone didn't take her? She'd never get into someone's car. You're right, she would walk off. I'll kill her.

Mal, stay with Doireann! Please keep your eye on him.

Mike, what'll I do? It's not okay. It's not. Where is she, Mike?

Oh, Mike, oh fuck! Oh Jesus!

Doireann, can you drive down that way?

I can't stay calm, Mike.

Oh God, I wish you were here.

LOLA. I don't want to stop walking because then I'll have to go home.

ROSE. The police have just gone. Nothing to do but wait. They were over to us within twenty minutes and were very nice though I can tell they aren't worried. But I am. I know Lyndsey. She's been working up to this for ages now but I didn't see it. So many things I haven't seen. Wasting time in front of mirrors to see is there any sign of me coming back when I should've been looking at my little ones. Lyndsey, please, please be okay and I promise I will never ignore you again.

LOLA. I did stop walking after I'd worn the path thin. I discovered a coffee shop which charges sixty cent extra for soya lattes. The manager wondered what all the fuss was about since I was having green tea. They just don't get it. So great to be dealing with humans again.

ROSE. Mike called every ten minutes. The police told us to stay put in case she came back. Doireann tried to distract Malcolm, but he just sat on my knee and hugged me like he was three again and said nothing. It's when it started to get dark that he whispered in my ear that he was sorry he didn't protect Lyndsey.

LOLA. And then I saw her.

What a beautiful fairy. She sat there crying her eyes out in front of a dreadful concoction – hot chocolate with whipped cream and Smarties, I think. So I asked her if she was all right –

LYNDSEY. I'm fine.

LOLA. and did she need anything but her / 'no'

LYNDSEY. No.

LOLA (*continuing*). was very clear and it was very clear she was not fine so I started talking to her. About how I love hot chocolate too though I wouldn't eat Smarties if you paid me and the chocolate has to be organic and it turns out her / mother eats organic –

LYNDSEY. Mam eats organic chocolate too, and I told her all about Mam and losing her hair and being sick. Can you imagine, a total stranger and I told her everything on my mind – how messy Malcolm's room is and how Tammy has the most gorgeous clothes and how Mam was supposed to go shopping with me. She didn't sit down; just stood there drinking her weird tea and finally I stopped and she let me use her phone.

LYNDSEY *rings* ROSE.

LYNDSEY. Mammy!

LYNDSEY *looks at* LOLA.

ROSE. Jesus, Lyndsey. Thank God. Where are you?

LYNDSEY. I'm in a café. This is Lola's phone.

ROSE. Who the fuck is Lola?

LYNDSEY. Stop giving out to me.

ROSE. Okay. I'm sorry. Just tell me where you are.

LYNDSEY. At Two for Tea café on the coast road. (*Pause*.) Okay.

ROSE. Mike, we found her!

I thought we'd never get there – to the café where the woman with the phone found my daughter, or my daughter found her. I didn't know which but I needed to sit down with them both. Her name is Lola.

LYNDSEY. Mammy squeezed me so hard I thought I'd break. Doireann brought Mal back to the car when he started calling Lola a witch. I think he thinks she kidnapped me. How embarrassing.

ROSE. I couldn't let her go. I couldn't let either of them go. So we talked. It appears the two ladies had covered a lot of ground. Lola invited us to her house for dinner.

LOLA. Archie, you'd have loved it. I finally had an adventure without trying. We always say those are the best kind. And though I've not been known for my spontaneous dinner parties, I'm having one tonight. Don't even care what food is in the house. We'll climb over the boxes and feast.

LYNDSEY. Doireann looked sorta frightened when we said we were goin' back to Lola's. She said she'd drive home with Mal and we could get the train whenever we wanted.

Lola has thirty-seven cats. Not real ones unfortunately but special ones. They're made of iron and they guard her. They've got spiders hangin' round their necks. Archie bought them for her. Archie painted so many paintings that their house is gigantic to try to fit them all. Archie wasn't there. It would have been a squeeze if he was – there's boxes everywhere. He's working overseas. He sounds great. Like my dad except older.

Lola let me take the cats out of the box and I arranged the cats in a big semicircle around her back door so nobody could get us. I gave Mam a really big fright. She was very upset that I went away. I promise I'll never do it again.

ROSE. I don't feel old around Lola. I feel alive or is that because I've found Lyndsey?

Lyndsey is in the kitchen, transfixed by Lola's ornaments. Lola hands me a glass of red and steps over a pile of clothes and sits into an armchair covered in more clothes.

Why is she looking at me? Maybe she's noticing my lack of eyelashes and eyebrows. If she is, she's not surprised like other people. I look away. You can't look at someone for that long.

Maybe this wasn't such a good idea. Then she said it.

LOLA. I had a double mastectomy.

ROSE. I looked at her. You can look at someone for as long as you like. When we did start talking, it wasn't about missing hair or breasts but about men.

LOLA. I told Rose how Archie and I met – the bird costume – everything.

That's how I knew he was able for me.

ROSE. When Mike and I were goin' out he used to speak to the cat out in the yard when he knew I was listenin'. I'd be putting on make-up in the bathroom and the window'd be open. He'd be waitin' outside for us to go to Roche's. He'd start talking to the cat and just say things like, 'Do ya think she'll take forever, Tabs?' One evening I was putting on me lipstick and I heard him sayin':

'I went all traditional and asked her father, now I'm mentionin' it to you, Tabs, what do you think she'll say?'

I dropped the lipstick and flew out the door, round the corner and leapt on him . . . We were only twenty-one, very young.

LYNDSEY. Mammy and I slept in a four-poster bed. I'm not jokin'. She hugged me for ages. I told her about the hair straightener and she said I was a divil and then laughed and laughed. I joined in and then we heard Lola in the next room joinin' in too. She didn't even know what the joke was so that made us laugh more and I'd say we all laughed till we couldn't laugh anymore.

The next day we went home and Daddy started to be cross saying, 'We'll need to talk about you walking off, miss.' But then I told him about me and Mam sleepin' in a four-poster bed, he said, 'Sure yer probably sorry to be back in that case.' I was going to say, 'Well yes, sort of.' when I saw he wasn't looking at me, he was looking at Mammy and she said, 'No . . . We're glad.'

Can't wait to tell Sophie.

*Lights, music and scene change again to depict change of time.*

*End of Act Two.*

## ACT THREE

### After

LYNDSEY. I now prefer Mammy to Daddy.

It all started and ended with Malcolm funnily enough. Mal was hangin' outta me so I gave him Kangaroo to play with. He can't reach it ye see. Daddy came in and said if I touch the Australia shelf again he'll increase the age for me getting a mobile phone.

Dessie brought Kangaroo home at Christmas one year and Daddy put him on the highest shelf with all his books and maps on Australia. For some reason we're supposed to treat Kangaroo like he's an expensive ornament.

All Mammy and Daddy's friends went to Australia when they were younger but Dessie stayed there. So I had a secret plan for when I'm grown up to bring Daddy over to Dessie for three months. Daddy says there's no point in goin' there for any less than three months but 'twould be better to go for a year. I don't think me private investigator wages would stretch to a year.

Let's just say my secret plan isn't a secret anymore because I told Daddy and warned him that there'll be no Australia if he messes with the mobile phone agreement.

Daddy hates threats so I didn't think it'd work very well but I can't be expected to control my temper all of the time.

Here's the weirdest part. He looked at me for ages and then hugged me. 'Twas only when we'd finished huggin' that we noticed Malcolm had snapped off Kangaroo's tail.

I rang Lola this evening and asked her if we could come and stay next weekend. She told me to ask Mammy. I knew she'd say no so I just said 'never mind' to Lola. But after Mammy had finished talkin' to her (for hours by the way) she announced we are goin' up for a night to see Lola next weekend. I can't believe it. Mammy is just so cool. I thought I'd never be allowed go anywhere again. And even better – Malcolm's not coming!

ROSE. Mike's not really speaking to me. I expect it's easier for him that way, more honest, I suppose. I stupidly thought that because we were so together when Lyndsey was lost that it'd remind him what we used to be or something. Anyway, it hasn't. I even let myself fantasise about it, maybe he'd run out to meet us when we came back from Lola's, maybe we'd hug. He was pissed off with me; I know he thinks it's weird that we stayed in Lola's. His daughter went missin' and then I took her to a stranger's house. 'You handled that badly, Rose.' Trust me, you asshole. I know he thinks I'm mad goin' to Dublin again. Himself and Doireann agree on something at last. She was drivin' me to chemo today and rolled her eyes when I told her Lyndsey and I were goin' back to Lola this weekend. Sorry, Doireann, I was under the illusion that you wanted me to be happy, or at least feel better. Fuck them. Fuck Mike. I've got a friend in Dublin, Mike. Someone who gives a shit. No more fantasies.

I went on the internet tonight 'cause I couldn't sleep and I'm so sick of television. 'Under the skin a 'tail' of breast tissue extends into the armpit (axilla). The armpits also contain a collection of lymph nodes (glands), which make up a part of the lymphatic system. The lymphatic system is a network of lymph nodes connected throughout the body by minute vessels called lymph vessels . . . ' Lily took a trip down the tail of breast tissue . . .

Fifteen minutes later I was on the phone to Lola . . .

I told her I Googled 'breast cancer' and 'cure'.

She said that was my first mistake.

227,000 links came up. The first site went on and on about how chemo kills all your good cells and leaves your immune system weak, and then the next link says 'look no further you have the cure for breast cancer already – your immune system . . . ' and then it went on to talk about building your immune system instead of having chemo, and chemotherapy is so hard on your immune system and that's the treatment I'm getting. Nobody told me all the options. I should have done more research.

LOLA. I told Rosey, if she'd done her research when she was diagnosed, she would've still gone for chemo.

ROSE. She said I was never going to be a trailblazer with two small children. But nobody even mentioned an alternative – and I read about this woman who has written a book about not eating processed foods and animal fats, it should be all organic and dairy-free. There's no harm giving it a try, but if I'd known before, why does nobody tell you? Then the next thing I read was this conspiracy theory about the companies that make pesticides that give us cancer also make chemotherapy drugs – is that true? I mean, do pesticides even give you cancer? And then, I know it's supposed to be a myth but, another site said that antiperspirant does cause breast cancer and underwire bras or if someone bangs into you.

LOLA. Stop! Stop speaking and turn off the computer. There is strong evidence to suggest that altering your diet can be good for your health and after that the main influencing factors are age, gender and family history. None of which you have any control over. The thing one must do is regularly check one's breasts and get any lumps seen to right away. You've done that, Rose. You've done everything right . . .

ROSE. Yes, but . . .

LOLA. It's not your fault, Rose.

*Silence.*

ROSE. I hung up, went to bed and fell asleep.

LYNDSEY. I feel sorry for Mal. I was delighted it was just me and Mammy but I thought Daddy would bring him to Tramore or somethin'. Mammy told Mal that it'll be his turn next for an outing but it doesn't work that way. The rule is: if our outings are separate then they have to happen at the same time. We always have them at the same time if we're split up. I'd hate to be left here with moody Dad. Mal isn't even kickin' up a fuss. I don't really want to go now. I'll ask Mammy if we can bring him.

LOLA (*speaking to Archie*). They'll arrive late so it'll be soup, salad, delightful chats and bed.

Saturday morning, Rose sleeps in. Lyndsey and I go to Dundrum shopping centre – she's never been. Then Seaview for lunch. Must show Lyndsey their delightful aquarium.

Back here in the afternoon. A little rest before they catch their train. Only two more sleeps till their arrival.

ROSE. Who's looking after who? Lyndsey is right. Malcolm should come because Mike isn't going to bother, but Malcolm will need to be minded and I want a rest. Lyndsey said she'd look after him. I am a rotten mother. Don't want to go now.

LOLA. Only one more sleep.

LYNDSEY. Mammy said Malcolm can't come. So I said I'm stayin' at home then. She just sat there lookin' sad and after ages she told me we'd all go another time. I think that means none of us are going now. I had told Sophie all about it. Going to pretend we did anyway. Sophie doesn't care.

There's nothing to look forward to.

ROSE. Lola was as positive as ever. Said it was no bother at all. We can come another time.

LOLA. I'm sentenced really. The slightest rejection – Rose not coming – and I imagine a million times, that's what you had, a million times what I'm feeling. I didn't know what else to do, Archie. I shut you out because I hated you for caring about me. I felt like I'd brought it on us and you were ridiculous to stay with me. I wanted to humiliate you into leaving. I'm glad you're still here, Archie, but I think you're here to remind me, remind me what I did to you. I'd haunt you too if you did that to me. Oh, God!

LYNDSEY. Tammy Flynn is best friends with Sinead O'Gorman. They played spin the bottle with boys from first year over the summer. First day back at school and already Tammy's showin' off. So Sophie is hangin' around me again. Lola said 'It's not about revenge, it's about self-respect,' so I'm giving her a trial period. It is our final year in primary school, so I should.

Sophie went to England and Tammy went to Majorca on holidays. I just went to Dublin for a night. It's not exactly a holiday.

Mammy's hair is growing back but it's still very short. She went for a walk up the fields today and when she came back she said she could feel a draft. She had lost her pretend boob on her walk. I was panic-stricken but then she laughed and laughed and held onto the counter and laughed some more and said she was chancing her luck and put it in the wrong bra.

Laughing is like yawning, it's contagious and Mammy hasn't laughed since Lola's. I decided to join in, and even stupid

Malcolm laughed and just for those few minutes I didn't hate him. We went up the fields in search of Mammy's breast and met Daddy on the way. He decided to help too. Malcolm found it covered in gravel by the stream like a dead jelly fish. When we got home Mammy washed it and Malcolm put a plaster on it, the stupid fool. Mammy kissed him on the head; oh God! I don't know how she does it.

ROSE. Limbo, nothing to do about Lily now. Treatment finished today. Didn't realise it was my last one, wasn't prepared. Elaine, the really young nurse, was taking the line out of my hand and wishing me the best. I looked straight into me mother's eyes across the way, she looked like she knew I wasn't ready to go. I held her eyes. Why was she still here? I hope she's okay, why didn't I talk to her? Then she nodded, that meant it's going to be okay, thanks, Ma. I followed Elaine up to Dr Mills's office, dried my eyes and watched his face while he explained my medication. Back to Doireann at reception. Didn't want to leave the hospital. Doireann bought me a hideous plaid shawl that probably cost a fortune. I know I'm supposed to be delighted but I'm not. Going to a hospital means I'm doing something crucial, important. I felt like going back and saying to Dr Mills, 'Okay, so I have my tablets but what else do you prescribe? That I cross my fucking fingers?' Definitely not trying to impress the doctors anymore.

What do I do now? Just hope Lily doesn't come back? Is that what I do now? For the rest of my life? Oh God!

LYNDSEY. Sinead O'Gorman is having a sleepover for her birthday and she invited Sophie but not me. Nearly all the girls in the class are going. Sophie said she won't go since I'm not invited. I told her she had just shortened her trial period and then we went to her house to see Mildred. Life can be just so surprising. Mrs Gallagher asked how Mammy is. My face burned. We've gotten so far without Sophie knowing.

ROSE. I have hair and resolutions – enough hair to look normal. It started growing back when they changed my chemo, peach fuzz at first. I couldn't believe it. I couldn't believe I'd lose it and then I couldn't believe it came back.

My resolutions: I haven't asked about Mona in a month, don't want to be obsessed with breast cancer anymore, no more day-dreamin', and I'm going to Dublin to see Lola every second weekend. I've been twice since we met her and it has done me the world of good. We went flyin' kites on Sandymount Strand. I felt foolish at first and then delighted. No small town watchin' me. Mike and Doireann think it's weird, me visitin' Lola, but I don't care. Lola makes me feel better. Mike doesn't make me feel better. I just can't think about that fact though, it's just too big.

Lola thinks I've managed really well. She's the only person who has said anything like that to me.

Everything aches but I'm keeping it to myself. Don't think I can keep on complaining now that treatment's over. Dyin' to go back to work next week.

LOLA. Archie, you would have painted Lyndsey's right sock hanging loosely around her ankle. It made me sad because . . . it's fleeting.

Both of them would almost make you sorry you didn't have children.

I know, I know, I can't blame you for that, but I did say 'almost'. There would have been less time for just us.

Unimaginable now.

We have so much fun, Archie. I hope they keep coming.

They're so different to your stuffy art friends.

LYNDSEY. When I woke up today it was raining which I suppose is the perfect weather for a funeral. I know this is a terrible thing to say but I felt kind of excited, even kind of happy but not really of course, all at the same time. I didn't cry at all, though Malcolm was crying when I got downstairs so I had to be cross so he would shut up and Daddy wouldn't hear him. I told him to get his things together. That I was in charge now.

At the last minute I got Mam's woollen plaid shawl. I know she wouldn't have minded. It's pink and green plaid. Doireann gave it to her. She got it in the Kilkenny Design Centre but I don't think I ever saw Mam use it. I knew it would be perfect for the funeral. So me and Mal walked and met Sophie at the end of our lane. She didn't say anything, just hugged me really hard even though that was really difficult to do because she was also holding the box with Mildred in it. When Mildred got run over by the car Sophie was beside herself. They wrapped the cat in an old blanket to take her to the vet but they couldn't do anything. So I took charge and told her I would plan the funeral and Sophie looked so relieved. She was far too grief-stricken to think straight. For one thing, that blanket had to be replaced with a nice one which is where Mam's shawl came in. I hope she doesn't go mad, though I don't think she can once she realises what it was used for.

Malcolm was still bawlin' which is quite embarrassing since he didn't know Mildred and he doesn't really like cats. I only let him come because we needed some music and he's quite good on the recorder. Unfortunately he only knows one song, 'Long, Long Ago', so he had to play it about eleven times while we buried Mildred. Then after we had Jaffa Cakes and tea that I brought in a flask. We sat on the tree stumps in the back field. We told Malcolm to go away so we could talk. Then Sophie said the best thing. She said we should get started on our Australia project for the end of the year that's if I still wanted to be her partner? And then I felt like crying because even though we've just been to a funeral I knew Sophie's trial period was over.

ROSE. I went into the salon today. It was busy. Dave made time. He asked to see my hair, then he asked me which one was fake. I told him to fuck off. I had just stepped outside when Doireann rang. Mona's dead.

She was on the way to her funeral. The funeral. Mona's funeral. The hubby says it went into her bones and it only took a few months. Doireann's tone said 'shit happens'. I hung up.

What about her three little Malcolms? How did she know it had gone into her bones? What was the first sign? What the fuck is happening? Just stood there. Paralysed. It's that fuckin' easy. Mona's gone!

Found me legs, got into the car and rang Lola.

I can't really remember what I said or how long I was onto her.

I do remember Lola reminding me that her cancer came back and she's still here.

And over and over again she said, 'No, Rosey, it's not fair, but remember we're all different.'

I'm here and Mona's dead and Lola has the energy of a small child.

LOLA. Rose and Mike are far far away from each other. Gorgeous Rose with her frightened eyes. She upsets me sometimes, you know, she sort of haunts me because she functions. She deals with the day to day, you can see it. She looks at me like I'm great and I don't contradict her, Archie. I don't tell her I didn't cope because I love that she admires me. I feel like myself around her. Rose never lies in the dark. I'm so truly sorry, Archie . . .

ROSE. I'm leanin' against Mike and Mike's leanin' against me. Neither of us are goin' anywhere in a hurry. This day started out relatively normal. I went back to work. Dave winked at me. Nobody made a fuss. I was so tired but I felt useful and right now there is no better feeling.

When I got home I'd an hour before the kids finished school so I checked our e-mail. I hadn't checked it in years. No more daydreamin'.

I opened the last one from Dessie, he's seein' a Japanese girl, got a raise and will never stop missin' proper Guinness. Then he said, 'I've read up on it, Mike, breast cancer is one of the best cancers to get.' What does that mean? 'She just needs time. It's probably easier to talk to women about it.' I re-read it three times. They were talking about me. I didn't think twice, I just scrolled down to see what Mike had sent him.

'R has finished treatment. She seems in better form. She keeps goin' to Dublin, maybe they fancy each other.'

Asshole.

I kept scrolling.

'She's so sick, Des', 'There's nothing I can do', scrolling, 'I don't want to confront her about anything when she's this wrecked', scrolling, 'She let me shave her head, I was so relieved.'

Oh Jesus, Mike . . . Why didn't you tell me you gave a fuck!

Scrolling.

'She excludes me completely; I think I was the last to know she was even sick. She can be so fuckin' selfish but it's still fair hard to see her do this on her own and havin' her sister, the devil-in-law around isn't helpin'.'

Prick!

'I can't believe this hippy from Dublin, Lola, she's getting her onto dairy-free – I'm a fuckin' dairy farmer.'

*She laughs.*

Scrolling.

'Not sure we're gonna make it through this one, Dessie.'

*Pause.*

I rang Lola.

LOLA. She told me about the e-mails Mike wrote. She asked me why he hadn't told her. I said, 'How would I know?' She actually attempted to answer me so I said, 'Only Mike can tell you that, Rose.' and I hung up. Hallelujah!

I know how to support her. I'm good at this. I rang a cancer support group in Bray. I'm joining them next Tuesday. I'm good at this . . .

ROSE. Lola hung up on me. I saw Mike out the kitchen window hangin' a gate. I miss his arms. As soon as I got into the yard it comes outta me.

Why didn't you talk to me, Mike, I thought you didn't care, you acted like you didn't fucking care.

He held my eyes, Mike doesn't look anyone in the eye for long, sorta threw me.

I read your e-mails to Dessie, fuck you, Mike, I did this on my own.

He said that was because I wanted to.

I didn't want to, you didn't ask me what I wanted, but you told Dessie everything and Lola, by the way, has been a friend to me.

Apparently, Dessie has been a friend to him.

You didn't get breast cancer, Mike.

He didn't know what to do.

Well, here's a hint – don't act like you don't care.

He says nothing. He knows I'm at least right about that.

I'm goin' back inside.

And by the way if you're feelin' excluded then include yourself.

Then he pipes up, 'This is goin' on long before breast cancer, Rose.'

Yeah, since you didn't get to go to Australia with the lads. You know, Mike, when Lyndsey was four and all our friends went to Australia and broke up with each other and went off to do Masters, I didn't fuckin' care 'cause I had you and Lynd. But you did. Do you know what? Go, go to Australia, go tonight if you want.

LYNDSEY (*tentatively*). Mammy was screamin' but now Daddy is. He's so angry. They haven't noticed me comin' in from school or lookin' out the kitchen window. My private investigator skills are comin' in handy.

*She jumps.*

Daddy kicks a bucket really hard and Mammy jumps.

He said that they both wanted to go to Australia when they were younger; they made a pact to go even if they have kids. I hope we go. Then he says that Mammy broke the pact when she had me. Mammy said it's too hard with children and I'd be cross with her only she's started to cry. I wish Daddy would stop shoutin' now that she's cryin'. He's mean.

He says that Mammy has been sulking for six years – no she hasn't – and that she thinks Australia is more important than her but he doesn't think that, he never did. What are they goin' on about?

Now Daddy's cryin'. Thank God we live on a farm and nobody can see this. He keeps sayin', 'Why?' I don't know what he means. I wish she'd answer him. Now they're sort of half huggin' and Mammy says, 'It's not this simple, Mike.' in a really tired voice. Oh no she better not be sick again.

ROSE. He's sort of giving me half his weight. I'm goin' to fall over if he doesn't stop. Maybe we're holding each other up.

LYNDSEY. The best part of today was after Mammy and Daddy started huggin' like fools, Mr Knowles drives into the yard with Mal in the back of the car. Malcolm told everyone in school today that Daddy's combine harvester went outta control and rolled over my aunt Doireann. He said it ripped her to shreds and all that was left was the feather thing that stands on her head but we were all too upset to get it from the mess so Mal did and brought it to her husband in Cashel so he'd always have it.

Okay, so he's mad, fine, but not really fine because I'm in the same school as him. But even worse than that Mammy and Daddy are actin' all sleepy and stupid and didn't say a word to him. If that was me they'd run me over in the combine harvester.

LOLA. The group in Bray are charming. Small – only six including me – two frightened Roses who've just fled the treatment nest, and three who have been diagnosed between three and five years ago. There was a bit of confusion when I arrived. I wondered if I'd end up in prison again for unworthy reasons. I had hoped with my five year anniversary badge and my experience supporting Rose that I'd be leading a group. A squeaky mouse on the desk informed me that 'Rachel' will be facilitating the group. Rachel, she went on to say, is a nurse and a counsellor. Rachel is a conservative dresser, I wondered if it reflected her attitude but she seemed to be very interested in all of us. They love me, they love how long I'm well. I bring hope. I suggested Sunday afternoon walks. Rachel reminded me energy levels vary. I said I'd do piggy-backs. They laughed. I wasn't joking. I was making a difference, however small.

I haven't been around that many humans and liked it in a long, long time. I would even go so far as to say they're better company than my horses.

They're all so honest – the worst part was 'losing my hair', 'losing my boyfriend', 'not looking like myself', 'telling my children', 'needing surgery but not chemo', 'the shadow – the fear of it returning'. Everyone understood the shadow.

The best part was 'my sixtieth birthday in St. Luke's, best birthday of my life', 'my husband and I have better sex than ever', 'I hardly worry about anything now', 'I've taken up skydiving'.

And then I told them about Archie. I told them I didn't cope. They listened, like velvet. Rachel said prognosis has improved since I got it. It would have been handled differently with me. Thank you, Rachel. Be conservative if you like, but that doesn't excuse my behaviour.

LYNDSEY. Lola sent me down this amazing bird costume for Hallowe'en. Sophie is really jealous so I'm goin' to help her with her devil costume. Mammy will spray her hair with red hairspray and Mrs Gallagher got her horns in McDaid's. I'm goin' to rob Mammy's red pointy heels and lend them to Sophie. Best friends do things like that.

Daddy's bringin' us around for Hallowe'en. It's always better when you've a bit of a group but Malcolm has decided after four years of goin' out that he's too scared to go out 'cause of the ghosts. Sophie's getting ready at our house. She's bringin' red lipstick.

Doireann's mindin' us tomorrow night. I wonder if she knows what Malcolm said, she mightn't prefer him if she finds out. Mammy and Daddy are goin' out for dinner. I hope they don't start shoutin' at each other in public.

ROSE. I don't know how I feel. It's been black and white in me head for so long I can't figure out anything. He suggested we go out for dinner the week after the Malcolm situation at school. It's like we're datin' again. Why do I feel like a bitch? I'm actually nervous about the dinner. I was goin' to wear my red heels but they're wrecked from Sophie draggin' them through muck last night. Doireann has bought me so much clothes and I can't bear any of them. Haven't seen that woeful shawl in a while. What'll I wear? Shit. Want to look nice. I've only one breast.

Everything is too low cut, everything!

Lyndsey sticks her head around the door. She feels bad about the shoes – that gives me an idea. We raid her wardrobe; I rob one of her baggy t-shirts, fitted on me, blue, nice, casual, jeans and my black boots.

LOLA. I told the group about Rose. About her and Mike going on a date. They didn't discuss themselves much, mostly Malcolm, poor little Malcolm. But then as the night drew to a close, Rose asked him because she had to. It was imperative. It didn't take guts; it simply fell out of her mouth.

ROSE. Do you still fancy me?

LOLA. Apparently he had never stopped.

LOLA *and* ROSE *and* LYNDSEY *come together. This is the first 'real' scene of the play.*

LYNDSEY (*handing* LOLA *flowers*). Happy housewarming.

LOLA. Tiny flatwarming, you mean.

ROSE. Do not start complaining about the size of this place.

LOLA. I'll do my best. (*To* LYNDSEY.) It sounds like Sophie passed with flying colours.

LYNDSEY. The funeral really solidified our friendship.

ROSE. Do you know how expensive that shawl was?

LYNDSEY. You never wore it. Anyway we have presents. Mammy!

ROSE. I'm getting them. We don't even know if these are the right ones.

LYNDSEY (*snatches package*). They're oil paints, for Archie.

LOLA *slowly opens oil paints and smells them.*

ROSE. Are they the right kind? Does he use them? I mean, we wouldn't know . . .

LOLA (*quiet for a while*). Oh, ladies, this is a great gift.

*Silence.*

Archie has been dead for three years.

*Nobody speaks, they don't know what to do.*

ROSE. Oh sorry, I thought . . .

LYNDSEY. He was overseas.

LOLA. I lied. I'm sorry, I make it sound like he's alive. I speak to him and about him all the time; you must have wondered why he wasn't there all the times you were.

ROSE. I didn't, actually. I thought he was working. I was more wrapped up in myself.

*Silence.*

You do talk about him like he's alive.

LOLA. Do you think I'm mad?

LYNDSEY. I'm gonna text Sophie.

LYNDSEY *leaves.*

*Beat.*

ROSE. I don't think you're mad. Well, maybe a little.

LOLA. When I got cancer I didn't cope well like you, Rose. I pulled the curtains and went to bed for a long time.

51

ROSE. When I coped it was because I had to, for the kids. I would have been exactly the same if it wasn't for them.

LOLA. You don't understand. I ignored Archie, shut him out, punished him, he never gave up. He kept mindin' me. When I was better we were okay again, he knew I didn't want to speak of what happened so we never did. We didn't mention it once. I never got to explain to him why I shut him out, I never said sorry, Rose. He died of a bloody heart attack.

ROSE. That wasn't your fault, Lola.

LOLA (*quiet for a while*). Then whose fault is it?

*Silence.*

I run things by him all the time. He knows all about you and Lyndsey and Malcolm and Mike.

Oh shit, Rose, he's still here. He's haunting me. I say sorry every day. Why is he still fucking here?

ROSE. Maybe he's still fucking minding you.

LOLA (*laughs*). I'm getting better though. For three years I've avoided his stuff, his art, his clothes, and now I've sorted and smelt every memory in the house. So easy to make your world small, stagnant. Not a good idea, Rose.

ROSE. I know.

LOLA. A little girl called to the door earlier this year, looking for sponsorship. She commented on my stagnancy and I practically frogmarched her out the door. She was seven. I've avoided our art friends for years but things are shifting; I went to a party last Thursday – Angela's. She loved Archie's work. We've arranged to meet next week to walk her dog, Lily. I can't wait.

ROSE *starts to laugh.*

LOLA. What?

ROSE. Nothing.

LOLA. You said you'd more news?

ROSE. I'm booked in for breast reconstruction on the ninth.

LOLA. Wow! A new boob for the new year. There's no stopping you, is there? You didn't mention anything before.

ROSE. Well, I knew you didn't get it done and . . .

LYNDSEY *returns, listens in, rolls her eyes and goes off texting.*

LOLA. No, you're right, I'm no expert on reconstruction.

You know, my main reason for not getting it done was – and is – comfort. I can run like a child. I was big, Rose, big, big.

ROSE. That reminds me; I got you a present too.

ROSE *rummages in her bag.*

LYNDSEY *returns.*

LYNDSEY. At last, you've stopped talking about breast cancer.

ROSE (*produces two tickets*). They're for Dolly Parton, in London!

LOLA (*jumps up and hugs* ROSE). Hurray, hurray, hurray, how wonderful, oh, Dolly at last! You'll have to do my hair.

LYNDSEY*'s phone rings, she answers it and moves away from them.*

LYNDSEY. Hi, Sophie.

ROSE. Lola, there's something else.

LOLA. I don't know if I can take any more.

ROSE. It's not for you, it's for the family.

LOLA. Phew!

ROSE *checks* LYNDSEY*'s not looking. She produces flight tickets.*

ROSE. Four tickets to Melbourne for Easter.

LOLA. Oh, wow!

ROSE. I haven't told him yet. I'm thinking we go over to Dessie for a fortnight at Easter and see what we think. I mean, it's most of our savings, he'll either leave me or be delighted. Shit, Lola, everything isn't sorted out at all, we haven't really talked about anything. I can't understand how he could hold back for so long, but he thinks that's what I was doing, but I was reactin' to him. I mean, it hasn't been right for years and I can't stop the e-mails runnin' through me head.

LOLA. But –

ROSE. But there is an ease since the fight, sort of relief –

LOLA. And what about love-making?

ROSE (*looking around for* LYNDSEY). Jesus, Lola.

LOLA. Well?

ROSE. The night we went out for dinner . . .

LOLA. Oh, wonderful.

ROSE. I hate that he doesn't like you.

LOLA. We can fix that.

ROSE. How?

LOLA. I'll come down to visit and have a glass of milk.

*They laugh.*

ROSE (*indicates tickets*). He might think it's too much. This is too much, is it too much?

LOLA. There's no such thing as too much, Rosey.

*End of Act Three.*

## Epilogue

LYNDSEY. I asked Mammy last night if I could get fake tan to top up my Australia tan and before she could answer Malcolm said he wanted some too. He's so tiring. Mammy laughed and shook her head, I think that's a no.

LOLA. At the end of the day I sit at my fourth-floor window and look down at Grosvenor Square. I call it my 'wind-down' session, unless Angela calls and then it's a drinking session.

Sometimes when the girls are up, Rose and I sit in the window and watch Lyndsey on the swing in the square. Rose tells me Lyndsey would be far too cool to go on a swing at home.

ROSE. Once I got reconstructive surgery I felt I'd come full circle. I'd always imagined 'full circle' meaning things going back to the way they were. I couldn't have been more wrong. The shadow is here now and it's here to stay. It's not always a bad thing, it can root you in the present like nothing else.

LYNDSEY. Sophie and I are presenting our Australia project tomorrow. I'm wearing my yellow tartan bra for good luck. It's going to be amazing. We're showing some of my holiday footage from Melbourne with a *Waltzing Matilda* soundtrack. Then we'll play my interview with Dessie on 'Living in Australia'. We also have a real boomerang to hand around.

Sophie has done very little work so she's going to read some extracts from my holiday diary in an Australian accent. She has recorded *Home and Away* every day this week. She's actually quite good.

LOLA. I stopped speaking to Archie when I left Sandymount and something strange started happening. Everywhere I go I see moments and details I know he'd paint, potential paintings . . .

ROSE. Still a daydreamer too, I can be flung back into memories at the drop of a hat. Mike says it's like I'm watchin' me own private movie – completely transported. But that's not always bad either. Today I was doing Mrs Gallagher's roots and Therese passed by – Therese from chemo. I don't know her but we were linked in a way not too many people can say they are. She didn't even see me but she threw me straight back in . . .

ROSE *continues, relives the memory.*

Back to that day in the chemo salon. Elaine had just put my line in. I put down the magazine. I know me mother across the way won't talk to me unless I speak to her first, and I really appreciate that. I people-watch. Therese is beside me mother and her husband always sits with her, their wrinkly hands laced together. They start laughing today and they can't stop.

LOLA. At first it was torture, paintings he'll never make, but now I take a photo and the moments aren't as lost as they were before. My apartment walls don many of them now. I have to be careful though. I'm quite the photographer and if the right people lay their eyes on my impressive shots I'll have *Art Today* knocking my door down. Everyone will want a piece of me.

LYNDSEY. After our practice today Sophie said, 'Your mam looks nice,' and I knew she knew, I wonder who told her, and I said, 'Mam always looks nice,' and she does. At the moment she has really curly hair and it's short so you can see her eyes better.

ROSE. It's a private joke, and they laugh like you do in school when you're going to get in trouble so that makes it worse. They look down, shake for a while and then come to a stop, but the second their eyes meet they're off again. I can't stop smiling. Nora with the wig-insisting husband is smiling too – it must feel unfair to her. Then the tears come, laughing tears dropping out of their eyes, and I notice Therese's cannula, the line of chemo pumping into her, it seems so secondary to the fun they are having.

It seemed so secondary because for that moment it really was.

*The End.*

**A Nick Hern Book**

*Unravelling the Ribbon* first published in Great Britain in 2007 as a paperback original by Nick Hern Books Limited, 14 Larden Road, London W3 7ST, in association with Gúna Nua Theatre Company and Plan B Productions

*Unravelling the Ribbon* copyright © 2007 Mary Kelly and Maureen White

Mary Kelly and Maureen White have asserted their moral right to be identified as the authors of this work

Cover photo: © Ros Kavanagh
Cover design: Ned Hoste, 2H

Typeset by Nick Hern Books, London
Printed and bound in Great Britain by Biddles, King's Lynn

A CIP catalogue record for this book is available from the British Library

ISBN 978 1 85459 571 3